BABE
IN THE
WOODS

SELF PORTRAIT

Yvonne Wakefield

Published by Pepin Enterprises, LLC
The Dalles, Oregon

www.YvonnePepinWakefield.com

Cover Design by Eric Labacz www.LabaczDesign.com
Interior Design by Tamara Cribley www.deliberatepage.com

For Anabell and Del

A Note from the Author

My story is recounted as truthfully and sequentially as permissible and corroborated by hand-written and published journal excerpts. All of the places and characters and events depicted in this work of nonfiction are real. The names of some characters have been changed or omitted to protect identifying characteristics and details of the living or the dead. Dialogue is drawn directly from my personal reference material and recollection.

Prologue

Bears had never bothered me before I shot one that summer on the mountain. As a borderline vegetarian, I reasoned, since I deliberately killed an animal I had to eat a bit of animal deliberately killed. Not entirely to restore karmic equilibrium, but so I could chew upon the carnal rush of slaughter.

On that summer day, when hummingbirds drilled air hot enough to bake vanilla smells out of ponderosa pine, I waited, primed to kill, on my log cabin porch. When a black bear parted brush and stopped midway in crossing the creek I grasped a thirty-thirty resting by my thigh. Leveled it on a two-by-four nailed across the railing, aimed, fired. The bear's eyes blew open in shock before it faltered, staggered upright and bolted in a tilted gait upwind of a bullet so immediately embraced.

Days after the bear had been found dead, I felt the need to eat meat to restore the cosmic balance knocked off kilter—a mere trigger squeeze is all it took. It had to be wild. Killed in the wild and not from the bear I shot. I bummed a frozen elk steak from a runty hunter. After it thawed I roasted the meat on a green willow stick over a twiggy fire beside the flashing creek, within spitting distance of where, only days before, I'd blown out a black bear's rib bone with a borrowed rifle at three hundred feet.

I seared venison until it was as brown as the branch piercing it. Until flames licked away and nearly blackened what cardinal red was left of an animal that like the bear had browsed, a season before, upon pale, green shivery shoots. When it cooled, I bit into that charred chunk and chewed.

The creek continued to flow. The forest practiced its natural order; every leaf, twig, pine needle, rock and pine cone in forested rapport. But the animal in me got all riled up and I choked up before I could swallow: swallow the fear that had taken us both down.

Miles above Oregon's John Day Valley, I felled, bucked, skinned, notched and chinked a log cabin together from trees: Douglas, red and white fir, and tamarack to classify a predominant few. I was a skinny 18 year old, fresh out of orthodontic braces when I began to rebuild the home lost four years before when orphan replaced the name of daughter.

The road leading to my backwoods home is so rutted and steep, even the most souped-up, air-shocked four-wheel drives lose traction in stretches named for disasters at these places. *The Eliminator* and *Shit and Slide* are but two.

Given the amount of rain or snow it is often swifter and safer to hike than it is to drive this road that ends beneath igneous peaks named after a blushing berry. I live here alone when I am not involved in occupations to bank income so I can buy time to live off the grid and ungirded. This log cabin is the only place I have to call home. It sits as empty as I feel when I am not there. There is no lock on the door.

John Day is a north-east central city sharing the same name with a valley, river, county and a dead trapper. Most of my close friends here call me Lavon. This mispronunciation twists off tongues conditioned to calling out the likes of women with names like Artice, Nadine, Emmeline, Delia or Octavia. Names solid as the pioneering women who lived up to them, unadorned with luxuries I take for granted in country where Yvonne just sounds too pampered, too proper.

Sometimes, depending on the work I'm bungling—tasks that involve steely razor-sharp pointy tools, trees and dirt—I will also answer to Dimwit, Addlebrained and Loser. Dumbass or Dumbshit occasionally interweave into my own self-calling. The summer I shot the bear I added Murderer to my list of nicknames despite the fact I was a conscientious objector and abided by Gandhi's teachings. One of his lessons is:

There are many causes that I am prepared to die for but no cause that I am prepared to kill for.

I've convoluted my practice of his philosophy by dispatching an animal I was not prepared to die for.

A rational impulse. Either a bear was going to get me. Or, I was going to get a bear. Who did who in first abet one's good fortune. A rifle greatly leveraged my winning odds.

On a pine-board shelf next to my loft bed, among erudite tomes and decades-outdated encyclopedias, is a hardback copy of *The Prophet*, the once-shiny cover now scuffed and dog-eared. I keep that book beside me when I sleep in the belief that dreaming beside Gibran's soulful words generates a token of divine light, like a halo surrounding this solitary life wrestling me to the mat. One passage is underlined and read again and again.

Your living is determined not so much by what life brings to you as by the attitude you bring to life; not so much by what happens to you as by the way your mind looks at what happens.

I am twenty-two. My family is dead. What I call home is a stack of logs in the Strawberry Mountains. My best friend is a cat. Out of principle for life, until I ate that venison I didn't eat furry things.

This is what I looked at.

1. The Telling Part

Four years before disturbing bears, I'd left behind a disturbed past, born with the deaths of my parents, and convoluted by foster care. The night orphan stamped my fate, I lay in bed wondering how I was going to survive until that first grief-soaked dawning. The next day. A month was too far off to envision a life lacking a familial foundation. Where and how I would live was unimaginable in this sudden freefall of abandon. Untethered in new darkness I had a vision—nothing woo-woo metaphysical, more like a Christ-less epiphany or maybe it was merely a wishful thought: When I came of legal age, I would build a cabin from trees, live there with a cat, make art, write poetry and drink Cold Duck. I had imbibed the sweet sparkling wine only once—a stolen sip from an adult's glass, left unattended at some wedding reception or funeral wake. I don't remember if the occasion marked joy or sorrow but never forgot how the sweet bubbles burst bother.

At age 18, in search of this dreamed property, in a roundabout way, I stopped in John Day, a rural city named after a long-dead trapper from Kentucky. Like his traveling pal Daniel Boone, John Day had also headed west in search of pelted fortunes. But while Boone found fame exploiting the wilderness, Day lost part of himself in a wedge of Oregon now bearing his name. Land where I answered the question *where*.

With the help of a realtor named after a bird and wearing a cowboy hat, I purchased (with funds saved during my parents abbreviated life times, and meant to fund my college education) an 80-acre spring-fed draw with serpentine slopes and old-growth ponderosa pine shaded by the Strawberry

Mountains. My experience with logs at that time was limited to miniature interlocking wooden beams inside an iconic toy cardboard box.

In six months, with help, learning to wield tools that tested and wore me to the mettle, I finished cutting, bucking and skinning trees into a two-story log cabin with walls chinked tight. In 1975, at age nineteen I answered the question *how* and moved into my dream home with a tortoiseshell cat named after a larch tree.

That first year on the mountain I removed my Timex wristwatch and learned to divine time by temperature and elemental outpourings in all degrees of moisture and magnitude. Built off the grid before the term was popularized, living without electricity, telephone or running water meant simply that.

Instead of turning on an alloyed faucet I turn on my legs, running back and forth, knees adjusting to the weight of buckets filled from fiddlehead fern-laced creek waters. Instead of dialing a thermostat, a Diamond match ignites tinder to flamey heat inside a stove of welded cast iron. Kerosene lamps spotlight the papery pages I read or draw upon into long, dark nights that begin after a cocktail hour I never toasted as an under-aged recluse.

By the time fall gave summer the boot, I was snug in my twenty-by-twenty-four-foot log cabin and my best friends were a chainsaw, poleax and a cat named Tamarack. It is built on a north slope and this means by October, daylight fades and evening begins at 4:30 p.m. By then I'm indoors, feeding flames and balancing ball-point cursive furrows on blue lines in notebooks or drawing out my guts in indelible ink. In between literary or artistic ramblings I nibble cheese and crackers while sharpening chainsaw teeth with a bastard file, a cat with mother-separation anxiety in lap.

In the first part of November, tamarack exchange their lush lime green for golden needles that fall away, turning these stately trees into contrasting x-rays against winter's filmy sky.

By the end of November, nights are cold enough to freeze a one-pound Tillamook cheese hard as a brick inside the aluminum Coleman on the porch. The cooler is brought inside. Outside, snow covers the road necessitating that I leave my vehicles parked two miles below the cabin. Town is thirteen miles away and getting there to buy supplies becomes a day-long event.

Before sunrise I layer an empty backpack with library books and dirty laundry. At first light I bank the stove with a large damp log, close the door then strap on waxed cherrywood cross-country skis. I slush and mush until the incline steepens, then ditch the skis against a pine tree. Hiking becomes a brisker means of negotiating shin-high drifts.

The three-quarter-ton 1962 Ford pickup, oxidized army green that I bought used from a rancher in a cow pasture is covered in the same amount of snow I just plowed through. The 1974, gleaming Blarney Green American Motors Gremlin, a gift from my grandfather purchased off the showroom floor, is totally buried.

The Gremlin could never make the grade to the cabin and, after November skies threw down snow blankets that covered the ground into May, neither could the higher-chassis Ford. However, chained up, the truck can make it to the county road that butts into a salt-licked highway leading to town. The Gremlin stayed snow bound until the day I drove it away from what had finished me.

To get to town that first winter on the mountain, I fumble off with freezing fingers the same icy tire chains hooked on four miles back, then drive the plowed asphalt road leading to places where voices articulate outside the ones in my head. The process of changing bills and coins for groceries and hardware leaves me at times short on words. Tongue-tied, I rush transactions in order to get back to the cabin where my conversational skills are more compatible with a cat and inanimate objects.

The cabin is furnished with family keepsakes; a maple rocking chair, dinette set, various straight- back chairs, oriental carpets, silver bowls and heirloom Japanese ceramics and cloisonne; fragile preciousness sits atop bookshelves, chiseled to fit log curves. Moved half-way across the country they are now arranged in a space seemingly incongruous to their last placement—an urban split-level home. A large white enamel kitchen sink, rummaged from a ghost town runs parallel to a wood stove. Simplicity surrounds the simple-minded.

When not working in the frosty forest to cut firewood, I spend long hours in these surroundings sitting in a mustard-yellow upholstered rocking chair, rhythmic before the fire hearth, turning pages. Tamarack is on my lap, kneading and nursing my lapel with teeth, pricky as his claws, until my shirt is soaked in a spot he claims as his feline mother's teat.

When snow blankets too high to work outside and winter silences the earth, I read out loud just to hear the range of a human voice beyond, "Quit it! You sucking little shit!"

At times I stand under snowflake showers and yell, "Is anyone home?"

Waiting for a reply, I shiver with cold the wood stove cannot warm away and take a hike or split wood. Anything to keep my blood pumping.

Other times I read out loud on the porch, one hand stuck inside my shirt, the other holding out a hardback classic penned by a Roman emperor long since dead.

"You have power over your mind—not outside events. Realize this, and you will find strength."

The words, hung inside frosty breath balloons, dissipate by the time I realize my damp flannel shirt is frozen stiff.

Thawing out before the hearth I reposition Tamarack on my lap and substitute a great book for a paperback. America's beloved cartoonist, Charles Schulz's, *Very Funny Charlie Brown!* is a romping page-turner compared to Marcus Aurelius' stoic tome.

By December I've read every book in my personal library, skimming through the classics, and have grown tired of repeating, "Quit it!" as I turn over the same page in one book, again and again, my concentration as shifty as the cat nursing my shirt.

By January the soul-shattering silence outside and the thundering babble inside my head leads me to ask, do I leave the cabin before I absorb into insipidity or strangle the cat who is, like me, a needy little suck?

I identify with that cat so well I quit talking to it because I know it knows what I am thinking. I am hearing voices too; a porcelain coffee mug tells me its hard life story. Together an apple and orange weave an incomparable tale. An antique Japanese vase cries about its displacement after one nuclear bomb exploding. Every single object in and around the cabin has a story to tell and I talk back in ink scratches.

Since the first snowfall I've grown increasingly myopic and can see how dull I've grown in living alone. The spirit that guided me to the mountain and the grit and spit fire that drove me to finish building what started with a vision was dying as fast as the snow was piling up. So, it came with soul-searching hesitation and months of being snowed in to realize I have to leave what led me to the mountain or be consumed by cabin fever.

Returning from the weekly supply run my loaded pack includes a free brochure illustrated with tiny pictures particular to a specific geographic spot on a map. A covered wagon marks John Day, and a black seal squats west on a pinpoint named Eugene and I think about how to connect those two incongruous images separated by a saw-toothed mountain range.

The coo-belly dove-gray sky darkens over the last quarter mile before I scale the snow humped porch steps and is black as a bat by the time I unload the pack in the buttery light of four flaming kerosene lamps. By then my thinking had settled into a thought…it was time to leave my woodsy home and try out a different spot for just a bit.

2. Trying on a City

At the start of January, I close the door on the cabin, its logs still seasoning after spring's cutting. Holding Tamarack in a burlap sack I shuffle down the snow-bound mountain, strapped into the same red backpack I shouldered up to this raw land, nearly a year—or what feels like a lifetime—before. If I looked back, I'd start bawling. Only years before a dream, that log cabin had manifested security reclaimed and it was hard to leave.

That first year on the mountain I'd grown to know every evergreen trail, nook and cranny. Cutthroat trout in the dipping pool and chipmunks in the wood pile counted as some of my most confidential friends. Leaving them meant I had to trust the regional tourist brochure on the car seat and its caricature leading me on to a friendless city. All I had to do—according to a man in a hardware store, was keep myself warm and fed.

A summer before a hardware store clerk had assured me of these self-preservation requirements after a convoluted line of questioning. His first question being, "Those for your husband?"

"No."

"Then what are you going to do with them?"

"Spike down notched log ends," I answer shifting the fifty-pound box of twenty-penny nails on the counter.

I was wearing cutoffs and tennis shoes, not Carhartt or Levi or cowboy or steel toed Timberlines like his regular testosterone encumbered customers. Curiosity surrounding the asymmetry between my comparably petite physique and my hefty purchase prompted the clerk's next inquiry.

"Where's your parents?"

"Dead." I answer his second unsolicited question. Consolidating with one word that both my parents were killed by the cure they sought in hospitals when I was a kid.

"Hey kid, I grew up orphaned too." The clerk leans into the counter, his belly bulging over his belt like bread dough ready to be punched into a manageable loaf. He adds, "Pretty much raised myself. As long as you're warm and have enough to eat, you'll be okay."

He looked at me like I should know what he meant.

I did.

I paid for the nails. Lifted the box myself, not to show him I could carry half my weight, but to show him I was okay.

Living in a backwoods home was proof that I could take care of myself. I was just not certain if I could keep myself warm and fed in a place without trickling creeks, ponderosa pine peaks, timorous finned and furred palm-sized pals.

After digging the Gremlin out, a good friend is my first stop on the way to Eugene.

Relieved to be out of the sack, Tamarack sniffs the arms of Jim, a chiseled, statuesque father of two toddlers who I hired to help me build my cabin. He will continue to help me out by caring for my cat until I return in the spring. With a covered wagon at my back, I aim the Gremlin toward a place sealed with uncertainty.

In Eugene I discovered a mossy, wood-stove gloomy university town mushrooming between the wave-laced Pacific Ocean and the clear-cut Cascade Mountain Range. But there was not a seal in sight at this spot on the map named after another dead, venturesome man.

I enrolled in a community college and found a place to live. A 1952 trailer bought for cash, calculating it was cheaper than paying rent and it could be sold so I might break even when I left this doglegged metropolis.

Like anything manufactured so long before and neglected, that trailer had its share of problems. A corroded metal roof needed tarry patching. The only regular movement in the bathroom was backed-up plumbing. The oil heater I could never spark to heat, with an outside oil tank I couldn't afford to fill, were beyond my handywoman skills and college student budget.

Logs I knew. They were round and smooth and I could carve and chisel them together to fit true. Working around things with sharp corners and written directions discombobulated me as much as figuring into a city.

Eugene's spongy climate seeped through the tinny walls further warping the birch paneling. The original burnt-orange shag carpet smelled like mushrooms. A space heater attached to an extension cord warmed the fungal air enveloping my ankles. Beyond this electrified sphere drizzly chill spilled fast as wildfire inside the trailer.

I yearned for the sure and constant warmth of the wood burner in my log cabin and the simplicity of taking a leak freely in the forest just as much as it pained me to live in a cold leaky can and to flush a colicky toilet. In an effort to create comfort in that trailer I layered on sweaters.

To simply *live* in a city, I was generating expenses never figured in the simple life I left at the cabin. To save money I let my car insurance lapse, parked the Gremlin on the shady side of the mobile home park and relied on an emerald-green Peugeot ten-speed for transportation.

Biking about on my second day in Eugene I was T-boned at an intersection.

"It's okay. I'm all right," I tried to console the hysterical woman driver crying down at me.

I was picked up out of the street by strangers and led into a music store where police arrived to write up a report that required my new city address. Numbers stuck to facades hadn't concerned me on the mountain. It was shiver and shadows that guided me home and signed my residence in the forest. That's why I could only recite landmarks—"There's a little brown grocery store on the corner"—to direct the officer who drove me to the trailer. Later that week an insurance man wearing a soft gray suit was called to those same numbers. He gave me a check to cover the cost of a new pair of Lee's, a tire and rim.

January through May, I peddled the newly trued Peugeot across town to attend classes where I was usually marked late. Not because I biked slowly, but because I dragged my feet to get to a place that graded by percentage points, not common sense.

I did not assimilate well into an educational environment that felt as unnatural as the overhead lighting. In florescent lit cubicles I penciled answers to tests that would never be given on the mountain. I was a wiz with a chainsaw and poleax but my cutting skills did not match my competency in math class. Nor did I fit in with collegial extracurricular clubs or in hubs of student camaraderie. On campus even in new jeans and a clean pullover sweater I stood out like a babe out of the woods, as skittish around people as once were the trout and chipmunks who tamed me.

After classes one day, I encountered a hobo while picking blackberries on gritty bushes beside the train tracks just beyond my trailer's folding doorstep. He was also picking berries, putting them with no delay into his mouth instead of a dinky pink plastic bowl like me.

He was "Real hungry," he said when I nodded his way.

After a few words, which did not include his name, I named him Hobo, because I assumed he was part of the pack of homeless men camping beside the railroad tracks beyond my trailer. Like others I'd seen by the blackberry bushes, this man was unshaven and wore clothes the colors of the rails he rode and the ground upon which he slept. I invited him in and prepared to entertain his hunger. Every egg in the refrigerator was cracked into an exfoliating Teflon fry pan, and served under a patchwork quilt of melted Kraft cheese slices.

Without delay Hobo, holding his fork like a dagger or a lifeline, depending upon one's etiquette perspective, attacked the full plate. "Yes. Thank you, ma'am," he said when I asked if he wanted another piece of bread.

I'd never once been called ma'am before and though flattered this is as far as my matronly generosity extended, because I did not offer to let him use the toilet. By the time he left I fed him all my food except for a cellophane sack of popcorn stored in the trailer's overhead cupboard. I knew people back in John Day who were willing to help me when I was still a stranger and it was they who had taught me to reciprocate the same. That night popcorn and blackberries set my place at the dinner table.

On the bike back from school the next afternoon I stopped at the grocery store, weighting my knapsack with sardine tins just in time for a different hobo who came to my door. He did not go back to the tracks as hungry as I found him.

The next morning as I headed out for school, I found yet another hobo pacing at a respectful distance from my trailer steps. Word spread fast down the line of vagrant men who lived in brambles bordering the rail line a stone's throw from my trailer. I never asked any of these men, who must have been loved if only briefly as babies, how they grew into men who ended up on the wrong side of the tracks. I did though give everyone who waited beyond the doorstep a can of sardines. My brother once told me that food should be the only thing given to people down on their luck. Giving them money, he had advised, when I first observed him handing apples and sardine tins to a destitute man in a grocery store parking lot, was likely to fund what had cost them their luck.

One afternoon, I answered an unexpected knock on the trailer door and a scraggly man backed away as I swung it open. He stood below the last step holding his right arm like a dying baby, rocking it back and forth and whimpering like a wounded toddler. He pleaded with me to take him to the hospital. On the landlord's side of the jamb I was framing worry and voiced my consternation to the doorstep stranger.

"How can I trust you?" I said, hugging my arms across my chest. He mumbled a reply, stared at the palsied limb and started to cry in snotty spurts. His rheumy eyes were glued to injury until he raised his focus to my face—a glancing blow that my sense of moral obligation failed to dodge.

He was only sniffling by the time the engine warmed and he kept his eyes fixed ahead in the passenger seat of the Gremlin I drove without insurance, which he also lacked.

At the hospital I helped him out of the car. He followed as I led him to the emergency room, a place I knew by my own accounts. Because the hand on his injured arm was swelling blue he had trouble holding a pen to fill out paperwork so I did it for him, confirming my diagnosis.

"His arm is broken," I nodded at the sterile receptionist and back to the man's tattered shirt cuff. Even though this man was disheveled and shattered, I knew he had an occasion to be clean and whole in the love of a mother if only for a birthing moment. This man could also be somebody's long-lost brother and so I treated him like one and gave him the last folding money in my wallet before leaving this man in the hands of care.

Only a day after dropping off the hobo at the hospital, I returned to the trailer to discover my own brother, sleeping like a baby under the doorstep's shady belly and mistook him for the bum he appeared. He uncurled when I kicked his boot sole, slunk out and stood brushing his jeans. Since I'd last seen Mark, his premature receding hairline had matured. Beneath his domed forehead was an attempt at a handlebar mustache and a bearded growth, splayed like semi-manicured squirrel tail below his chin. I invited in my not-so-long-ago-lost brother.

"Nice place," he said looking around the cramped space, though we'd both been raised in a nuclear family proper and in much more plush and polished places. "Mind if I stay a while?" he asked, drinking sardine oil straight from the razor-edged tin, refusing the fork and china plate I extended.

Mark bunked down, unrolling his sleeping bag on the living room floor, just three feet from the kitchen refrigerator. The first night he plugged up the toilet.

"Buy a snake," he said, describing it. And I did, the next day at Ace Hardware, adjusting to its hard coil through my fabric knapsack as I biked home from college. That night, I watched my brother ream out the plumbing.

The next afternoon I cut algebra class and returned home early to find Mark outside the trailer drinking Jack Daniels with two unfamiliar hobos, empty sardine cans littering the pavers.

Late next afternoon, I returned to the trailer to find Mark gone. There was a note taped to the snake: *Always wind it back when you're done.* On the kitchen counter another note was tucked under a nearly drained Jack Daniels bottle: *Traded you for some sardines.*

By the end of May I was more familiar with hobos than Eugene's academic or social circles and I was itching to get home. On the mountain, wildflowers would be having a hoedown. Spring run-off would send the creek frothing against its banks, welcoming as a Labrador's ecstatic slobber as it greets its master home. Goshawks and magpies would be scratching hieroglyphs in the blue, blue yonder and I needed to join in this wild party and run. Run wearing only moccasins.

In Eugene, when I wasn't biking across town or feeding guys down on their luck, I was sitting under fluorescent lights in white rooms with sharp corners and other dimwits like me.

During a typing test in journalism class—so many words per minute with only five mistakes—my wheeled desk chair rolled back and the IBM Selectric fell in my lap. The typewriter was electric and my senses were not. I re-tested on a manual Olivetti and barely passed.

It was early June by then, final grades mailed and time to leave this self-imposed academic spell. Turning my back on a seal on a map I headed to a point pictured by a covered wagon.

3. Diversion

Back at the cabin, I poked around with hand tools, chainsaw, pencils, pens and paintbrushes and cat talked with Tamarack in this pretentious-less, self-imposed isolation.

Just as I'm getting friendly again with this solitude a new friend appears out of the blue with a bottle of Boone's Farm Strawberry Hill and inadvertently changes the course of my introspection. I'd met Shelly in an American Literature class in Eugene. She turned a poem I wrote into a song, pitched to the likes of her trilling heroine Melissa Manchester. The first refrain began, *Driving down the road, on the way to my log home, I swerve by a magpie met up with chrome...*

Before I left Eugene, I'd given Shelly a penciled map along with my mailbox address and she vowed to visit me at the cabin. She was driving to attend a three-day women's festival in Northern California and I am a detour, albeit out of the way. She extends an invitation to join her. Given my crammed social calendar it's not hard to fit an unplanned trip.

The next morning, I follow Shelly to a redwood forest swarming with women in all states of wonder and dress or undress.

As a native Californian I'd been in the redwood forest many times but I'd never seen it like this before—hundreds of women in all shapes and colors, communing under old-growth canopy. There are signs tied to trees indicating the staging grounds for workshops in Tarot, macramé, herbal tinctures, and yoga. The only one that interests me is Drawing.

Penned in flawless calligraphy, it is the classiest sign in the forest. The workshop is taught by a tawny, fortyish illustrator. Sporting coifed blonde hair, she appeared as out of place as her would-be protégée. Neither of us wore tie-dye or long skirts and we introduced ourselves with birth names rather than nature nicknames like Berry, Moss, Root or Cedar.

"Leona," is how the illustrator introduced herself to me.

She thumbed through my sketchbook and liked the pen and ink drawings I'd done of flora, creek, and mountain views. After a slight and welcomed critique—line, contrast and pattern—Leona led me to the camp's kitchen. There she liberated a bowl and a plate from a rough board shelf and told me to trace around them, then to go into the forest and fill those peripheries with whatever I felt like drawing.

Three sunny days of communing with Rapidograph pens under a canopy of old-growth cedar, filled a sketchbook with pen and ink drawings that brought me home to myself again.

Leona was not only a remarkable illustrator, she was also a recent divorcee with a young daughter who had relocated from Los Angeles. She planned to build a house on rural land not far from this gathering.

We made a deal. She would teach me illustration techniques in trade for my woodworking expertise, which was limited to chiseling curves and shimming level. Qualifying me, I was blustering sure, to help Leona build a house with exacting measures. It was a spur-of-the-moment decision that meant I would move to Mendocino, California. But I trusted my feelings and this mother who, like me, held on to her name.

I'd barely seen Shelly since we arrived at the women's festival. She was busy mixing herbs and mushrooms. When I told her, "I'm leaving," she had little to say beyond, "Ummmmm."

In Eugene I cancelled the next semester's enrollment, arranged for the sale of the trailer and with the proceeds later bought a used Datsun 1600 series truck with a locking camper shell over the bed. My time away had stretched into nearly a week and when I returned to the cabin there was still food in Tamarack's dishes but no sign of the cat.

For the rest of that summer I searched and called day and night for Tamarack under trees of the same name. My daily chores of splitting wood and hauling water were not the same without his fur shadowing. At night when I read, my lap was empty and my shirt front dry. Finally, I had to leave the cabin battened down for winter and move on without my best friend.

Northern California redwoods don't ooze vanilla sweet like the ponderosas holding my place on the mountainside. These coastal conifers weave dense blankets laced with iodine mist, surf, sand and shell.

The cabin 600 miles in my wake, I park the Datsun in a meadow beside a seasonal pond ringed by second-growth redwood trees. This meadow is a short walk from Leona's building site, which itself is a gorsy inland mile from the Pacific Ocean. For the time being the little truck will be my mobile home. A single burner propane camp stove, Hurricane lamp, sleeping bag and pad make the truck bed livable. A plywood plank, balanced between the gunwales, makes it workable. After a day of posturing as a carpenter, I either draw in my sketchbook or peck upon my garage-sale typewriter in the evening and into the night. I'm sheltered under the flimsy camper shell, the hinged hatch open to vent fumes until the lamp is blown out.

My days in Mendocino are pretty similar to my days at the cabin. From eight until three or four in the afternoon I do physical work, helping Leona frame her house. Under her direction I measure and saw accurate lengths and angles. This first time I built alone is the reason people over six feet tall stoop a bit when entering the front door in this little home, which would be more true and level if I'd never helped her to build it in the first place.

After a day of building Leona critiques my drawings from the night before, points out corrections and suggests new techniques. Problems identified, I return to the meadow, boil water for tea and eat Triscuits and cheese. Sitting-cross legged on the tailgate I draw from my mistakes. When it grows too dark to see or the fog rolls in, I retreat inside the camper and prime and ignite the Hurricane borrowed from the cabin.

Before blowing out the lamp I wrap my sketchbook in a plastic bag. By morning moisture is dripping down the thin sheet-metal walls, my sleeping bag and skin as slick as the bronchial cough settling in since the first night I bedded down under a maritime air mattress. The truck canopy offers only protection from rain and the heavy coastal fog that sometimes rolls in so quick and thick a person could get lost walking outside in it. I knew this as fact.

4. Holiday

Leona's house was progressing along with my illustrative skills, both timed by daylight that took a westerly hike too soon after September turned into October. After work If I wanted to see to read, write or draw inside the camper shell I had to light the Hurricane at 5 p.m. By the damp month of December, I could not keep the hatch open to vent kerosene fumes because of the saturating fog. This meant either working by flashlight in the evenings or bedding down early under a pea soup blanket.

Just before Christmas, the house was framed, paneled and roofed. There was still finish carpentry to complete but it was the holiday season and Leona left for Los Angeles. This left me alone in the stump meadow on Christmas Eve and destitution enough to negotiate hairpin turns in soggy, bluff-hugging mist to fulfill a vision of a hot restaurant meal in Mendocino.

When I arrive I discover the seaside village dim, streets congested with low-lidded haze instead of rosy-nosed carolers. Even the usually effervescent Seagull Inn—where I imagined myself seated at a white-clothed table—is closed.

Left to my own devices, I walk along the boardwalk then duck down side streets where pole lamps ensure I can find my way back to the truck. The Point Cabrillo Lighthouse moans due north. Ocean waves churn and crash against the headlands; my wheezy breathing times my wandering pace. All of this pushes my holiday melancholy to the brink. I usually begin dreading the approach of Christmas beginning in August. Now, facing this gloomy funk full on, I am playing a soul-sucking round of *Poor Me*. The solitary game of *I Don't Have a Family*.

When my family was alive, so was the holiday. There were cookies and fruitcake; presents ringed a Christmas tree that twinkled with tinsel and lights. Polished ornaments mirrored familial festivity.

After my parents died, the Grinch stole everything including my comfort and joy in this holiday.

Since then, I have enjoyed Christmas season as a stray—invited into reveling family homes because I'd not one of my own. Pitying do-gooders dragged white elephants from upper closet shelves, dusted off and re-gifted them so I wouldn't feel left out as others tore into name-tagged presents under a trimmed tree. I smiled and feigned delight from outside circles of good tidings as I unwrapped a used bottle of Avon perfume, a Santa-faced mug, or a cookbook inscribed, *For Joe: Here's Cookin at You! Love Bev.*

Now, on my first Christmas in Mendocino, no one invites me to join them. Not even a white elephant.

A row of weather-beaten, and restored Victorian homes line half a block beyond the village's seaside heart. Elegant burgundy drapes are tied back with golden tassels and I can see classy-dressed people inside house after house, laughing, eating and drinking while I shiver and stare. I am an outsider looking in and playing the *There are People Worse Off Than Me* game. I remember hungry, lonely people. People without a warm bed. People suffering from flesh and bone-eating diseases. People all over the world who are worse off than me. I am all of these people as they too are part of me.

Still, I cannot wiggle out of feeling like a twisted Oliver Twist. Nor do I want to lie curled in a pickup bed on Christmas Eve to rise to an equally dismal morning.

I turn my back on those cheery frames and trail fog until I am beside my truck. Once inside I start driving.

The Datsun makes it all the way to a twenty-four-hour truck stop in Redding before the fuel gauge needles over red and the thermos is empty. The only person inside is a cashier openly drinking Budweiser in front of a sign advertising the same.

"Whait a minute. Fesh pot e'll be ready in a jish." The young man, with two front teeth dark as the stubble on his chin, sets down his beer to fumble a paper filter, fill a glass pot with water, and pour it through the top of a humorless commercial coffee machine.

I wait drip by drop for a refill. The cashier hums along as Silent Night pipes through racks of beef jerky, sunflower seeds and Sugar Babies nestled in yellow cellophane jackets. His skin is cadaver-colored under twitchy fluorescent lights, his facial capillaries as lit up as the neon sign behind him. With a final hiccup and hiss, the glass pot is filled then mostly emptied into my Looney Tunes thermos—one cherished possession the Grinch missed.

Christmas Eve turns into Christmas dawn as I drive on, stopping only long enough at another twenty-four-hour gas station to pee and top off the truck and thermos. The cashier in Lakeview returns my change with another "Merry Christmas," but his good tiding is not slurred by Budweiser. His greeting is as sober as a reply that died along with my family. Deep down I know a response is in order but I cannot muster one. Uttering those two words back might crack the glue holding me together along a frozen asphalt artery where I hang onto the belief that I can outdistance the traction of not belonging.

Headlights bounce off snow berms—the only beacons of light in sight— until another sign reflects back a name, direction, soft drink, snack food, or some convenience so many miles ahead. I keep the radio off purposely, knowing only lachrymose carols will be courting the airwaves. The orchestral arrangement of engine whine, tire scrunch, and my coughing is harmony enough to keep me awake through a gray dawning.

At sunrise, a state patrol car tails me. I hold my breath waiting for flashing lights and to be pulled over for exceeding the limits of loneliness. When it passes in the left hand lane, I exhale in relief and think, *Maybe I should swerve and cause an accident.* There's a small chance the officer would turn back to save me. Most likely, though, I'd end up stuck in a ditch, the patrol car miles beyond my attempt to solicit human interaction. Then I'd have to save myself. Again.

Later a Frito Lay delivery truck whizzes by in the opposite lane. *Poor guy. Working on Christmas day.* At least he was getting paid. That's more than I am getting as I watch the fuel needle fall.

Normally it's an eleven hour drive, but I've been on the road a lot longer by the time I make it to John Day. The streets are as dead as the trapper the city was named after and I cruise through the town's only stop-light—actually the only stoplight in the entire county. It is not even turned on when I hang a right on the last stretch of an icy and slushy road that has slowed me down since Wagontire, a speck in the eye of a town. The final leg of road is under three feet of snow. No match for the Datsun. I park beside my other snow-bound truck.

Because I plan to stay at the cabin just a few days I shoulder only a day pack, pouchy with tidbits bought at truck stops along the way. The cabin is stocked with dry goods—oatmeal, powdered milk, legumes, raisins, a fresh jar of Tasters Choice and everything else I need, except a needy cat. I leave the emergency brake off so it doesn't freeze stuck and start walking.

Each step recalls past seasons tramped. Spring thaws melting into wildflower prisms and wavy emerald grasses. Summer's freshets, autumn's rusty plants and winter's monochrome skies pulsing with lattices of naked branches. And snow, erasing every land-locked color except evergreen boughs. Each step pumps blood back into legs crumpled for hours under the dashboard. Now the forest hush serenades me in place of piston precision. I take a shortcut over a ridge, knowing the snow will be deeper but the distance shorter.

By dead reckoning, I hike to the exact point where a barbed-wire fence sags, a tried and true passage. I belly through this familiar opening by pushing one wire down with my foot and raising the other with my hand, like jawing open a giant anaconda's choppers.

The knapsack snags on a steely fang but I wiggle free and bolt upright at the sound of branches cracking. I'd encountered deer on this stretch before but they merely coughed and sprinted high, snapping twigs in their primal retreat. Whatever is parting the forest now sounds dainty as a bullied elephant breaking free of Barnum and Bailey. When a brown horse explodes through an evergreen thicket, followed by a resounding "Mother fucker!" I know I am home.

It turns uphill when I wave my orange knapsack and kicks up snow alongside a canal dug by pig-tailed indentured servants over a century before. The horse is followed by my shouting brother. A rope is limp in his hand, his attempts at lassoing the horse as foiled as the rights of Chinese gold-rush laborers.

"Merry Christmas!" I holler back at my brother, really meaning it. Mark looks up, surprised as I am to find family in the wilderness on this holy day. Our only communication is through a mailbox on the county road. We never know who is coming or going unless one of us posts a letter or note and the other, by chance, is in the vicinity to read it. The mailbox was empty when I checked it on the way up so I assumed the mountain would be too.

"Fuckin' horse," my brother steams, his mustache dripping with condensation and snot, his nose red as the bandana tied around his neck. His brown cowboy hat is as scuffed as his ice-tipped boots. In jeans and a matching denim jacket, he looks the part of the buckaroo he is playing.

I learn Mark has been living in the ratty old shack I lived in for a while when building my log cabin and he invites me to join him for a Christmas dinner he is preparing.

"Bakin' a turkey. Stove's so hot the place is like a sauna," he says through a snotsicle rimming his furred upper lip.

Red Vines, Sugar Babies, enervated coffee and Dr. Pepper had sustained me on the road here and made any type of food seem more nourishing. Plus, sweating in a drafty vermin-infested cabin with my brother sounded divine compared to cheering on the holiday alone in my log cabin, sucking on leftover licorice.

It would be pitch black by the time I hiked back up from that turkey dinner. But the moon would be nearly full I was sure, as I'd chased it down the night before. There was still plenty of light left for me to prepare for the night ahead.

The temperature is colder inside the cabin than outside. Even the newspaper next to the stove is too frigid to easily ignite with matches I have to warm in my butt pocket before they'll strike. Eventually I fan a peevish teepee tinder fire into roaring flame that makes the stovepipe creak and hope there are no creosote chunks clinging inside to set a flare.

I scuffle underneath the cabin to get water buckets.

A wigwam of bark, sticks and mushrooms, reeking undeniably of pack rat, mounds against two overturned pails. I pick them up by their handles and kick apart the pile, scattering the nest, surprised to see teeny blue china pieces of the child's tea set kept on the window sill inside the cabin. Glinting in the middle of this dark mess is my silver baby spoon—*Yvonne* inscribed in the handle—two quarters and chewed pieces of aluminum foil. There is not a pack rat in sight.

Maybe they enjoyed high tea, left a tip and, like snowbirds, headed for Arizona. I doubted it. From experience I knew those stinkers would be back too soon and rebuild a nest bigger, more commodious and reeking than the one I'd just busted up. I pocket the quarters, reassemble the tea set on the book shelf and drop the spoon in the sink. It is now warmer inside the cabin than outside, at least beside the fire that is ready to heat water.

Icicles hang like fangs down the creek bank and frosty petticoats skirt boulders. I scoop up two buckets of water only a degree warmer than the snow, accidentally wetting my leather chopper and instantly changing the temperature of my hand to that of the creek. Inside the cabin I throw the soaking mitten on the hot stove top where it hisses and steams, flip it about then set it behind the stove to dry while I prepare for the night ahead.

I make sure enough firewood is stacked on the porch, with at least one fat chunk to bank the coals, then ensure kerosene lamps are arranged, mantles off, directly in reach inside the door. When I return from dinner with Mark, I'll ignite those lamps with a match also statically placed. The damp log used to bank the fire will be rolled over and embers stirred to cast more light on a hot water bath that was, only hours before, running with ice. These are rote rituals in what it takes to live efficiently in a wilderness cabin. With everything at the ready it is time to join a party I had, only the night before, watched in the company of fog.

The post-solstice moon is bright enough that I can hike without a flashlight a half mile slope I know by heart to this ramshackle relic I lived in briefly while building my cabin. With no foundation, the walls kind of wave instead of stand straight. There is so much Visqueen stapled over the rafters, the plastic sheeting presents more of a fire hazard than a barrier against leaking elements.

"Merry Christmas! Ho, ho, ho!" I yell from the door jamb—the groaning hinges three times older than me. Mark is sweating over a bowl, mashing potatoes, his face glistening from the heat of the cherry-hot wood-burning stove.

A small Christmas tree—there are a gazillion of them growing like weeds on this mountainside—is propped up by rocks on the far end of the room. Six surrounding kerosene lamps, serving as decoration, are as lit up as my brother.

"Here," he sets a thick crockery bowl of mashed potatoes on the counter and holds out a bottle. I take a swig and Jack Daniels instantly burns through the escalating cold in my chest.

Every twenty minutes Mark stokes the stove with six-inch tamarack splits, the coals within the firebox brighter than my orange knapsack.

I'm relaxing into the mellow glow of this family night when Mark stands and spits on the cookstove top. Timing the hiss of the saliva evaporating, he determines his bird is cooked. Using his sleeve as a hot pad he pulls the pan from the oven, sets it on the counter then jabs the breast with his Buck knife.

"See there's no pink. No chance of getting salmon vanilla poisoning." He points to a gash, wipes the Buck knife blade across his jeans, folds and returns it to his hip pocket.

"Just a minute." He goes outside and returns as quickly with a bottle of Mateus.

We'd been drinking that brand for years, before we were old enough to buy it. Our palates immediately developed a taste for the fizzy sweet the first time we pilfered a bottle and drank it on a golf course one Minnesota Christmas Eve, six years past—the first holiday we would celebrate without our parents dead frozen as the green beneath us. We could drink case after case of Mateus and it would still not be enough to drown the sorrows we choke back.

"You got a corkscrew?" Mark asks.

"Wait a second." I pull the Swiss Army knife out of my knapsack, hold it up to a lamp and unfold all the blades. "Nope."

Mark opens a drawer and pulls out a hammer and rusty spike he taps into the cork. With a final smack the cork is pushed inside the bottle and the lip cracks.

"Careful you don't drink any glass," he says, brushing off green fragments with his sleeve.

I reach up into the cupboard and dust off two lead crystal goblets, remnants of our mother's wedding trousseau which have managed to make it safely out of heated storage to land, unbroken, on a shelf in this pestilent place.

"Merry Christmas," we say in unison, raise our brimming glasses of sparkling wine, and in the same beat lower our eyes. Not because we are on the lookout for gut-piercing shards but because the toast is a razor-sharp reminder of what we lost and will never have again—a lifestyle with experiences once whole and bright. Now we are fragments of what is left of a familial foundation.

I'm sipping my Mateus and thinking that maybe, just maybe, our parents are looking upon us with good tidings, when out of the corner of my wandering eye I spy not one but two pack rats scuttling across the rafters.

In the blink of an eye Mark pulls out a pistol, holstered on his hip under an open flannel shirt. A report sharp as breaking crystal cracks my ear drums and Mark fires a second round.

"Fuck. Missed the bastards," he clicks on the safety and re-holsters the gun I hadn't noticed.

Nonchalantly he rises, opens a cupboard drawer and takes out a roll of duct tape and cotton batting. He stuffs cotton into two fresh bullet holes blasted in the side wall, covering them with duct tape—the repair job matching a half dozen more festooning that end of the cabin.

"I'll paint over it later," Mark explains.

I shrug my shoulders, my ears still ringing from the first and second report of what my brother is becoming.

While the turkey cools and the mashed potatoes stay warm and gravy bubbles on the stove top, Mark climbs up the ladder into the loft and returns with a box.

"Here." He holds it out to me.

Sorrel Women Size 7 and what is printed on the outside of the box is true. Two sizes too big for me, the boots offer more insulation than the mink-oiled, bear-greased-and-buttered, size five Raichles I wear through all seasons. With a couple of extra pairs of socks and cinched tight at the top, these boots are still a loose fit but represent a true measure of what my brother can be.

"Was saving them for your birthday. Didn't expect you to be here for Christmas." Mark returns to the stove, stirs the potatoes, licks the masher. "Needs more butter." He peels the paper wrapping off an entire stick and throws it into the pot, unscrews the lid on a saltshaker and adds a hefty shot.

"Dark or light?" he asks hacking apart the bird with his Buck knife, refusing to use our mother's silver-handled carving knife I've extended. There is a second bottle of Mateus and thick brownish gravy begins to pour forth from a gold-gilded china spout.

I have two servings of potatoes, sculpting each scoop into a cauldron where I imagine the giblets are Christmas elves doing the backstroke. "Good gravy," I say to my brother.

"I think so too." Mark looks up from gnawing, grease from the drumstick slicking his mustache.

"Almost like mom's," I add, which ends our satiated chatter. We assume a silence as we chew on memories reignited by the tink-tink of family china.

Despite no parents to guide us through adolescence, we survived and retained some modicum of our family values and some family possessions too, like the silver, crystal and bone-china plates poised on our denim-covered laps. That night we eat until we are full yet there are parts in each one of us that will remain eternally empty; the aftermath of death scoured us to the core.

When Mark finishes a third helping, he sets his plate on the counter, knife and fork perpendicular, the way our mother taught us. He stands, walks to the door and before opening it turns and says, "I've got a surprise," and leaves. I'm heating wash water when he opens the door, his nose rosy from the cold outside.

"Get your coat on." And like I was born to follow my older brother's every command, I trail him out into the night.

The horse is tied to a tree and harnessed to a sleigh. Actually, it's a refrigerator door spiked and wired into two two-by-fours that serve as sleigh runners.

"Built it so he can haul his own hay. Haven't tried it out yet though. Get on." I sit down on the metal door like I never question my brother's half-baked inventions.

"Have one for the road," Mark hands off a half-pint of Wild Turkey from his jean jacket pocket, then adjusts the makeshift rope harness.

I take a sip then another to feel the burn I'm hoping will kill whatever is eating my bronchia alive. It's not this clean mountain air but a culmination of coastal fog and damp nights, in a truck bed as frigid as the icebox door beneath my butt.

Keeping his eyes glued to the horse's backside, one hand on the slack rope reins, Mark gropes for a seat.

"Hang on!" he says not even twisting his neck to acknowledge his passenger.

Instead of holding him around the waist I grip his jacket pockets and feel awkward in more than one way, plastered against his back. The last time I was this close to my brother was the night our mother died and our shaky embrace was inspired by retching loss, not in anticipation of a ride like this.

Mark throws a half-baked snow ball, overhand, girly-like, but with all the force he can muster from his perch on the refrigerator hatch. The horse takes the blow and bolts, causing the sled to lurch. The two-by-four runners pierce the snow and the lid upends spilling us into the snow. Holding tight to the rope, Mark is dragged like a rag doll up slope, all the while screaming "Whoa you mother fucker! Whoa!" as he body surfs into a snowy Yuletide night.

5. Happy New Year

The next morning I wake, like the interior logs, all snug and toasty, compliments of the consistent, reliable, wood-stove heat. But all those months of breathing coastal fog have embedded in my lungs and I can't shake the bronchitis brewing in my chest for as long as I started sleeping in a truck bed.

I stay in the loft all day and cough up phlegm tacky enough to repair a few loose chinking patches, if the desire was there. The only inclination to unravel from my blanket cocoon is born of necessity to use the outhouse, the seat cold as the refrigerator door that vaulted over me only the night before.

By late afternoon I'm bored sick with being balled up in a coughing fit. Downstairs, I sit mummified in a blanket in front of the fire until footsteps on the porch punctuate my crouping. My brother flashes by the window, opens the door and steps inside. I do not offer to get up and make him a cup of coffee I am too ill to stir up for myself.

"Howdy. I'm leaving for Vail." He wipes his nose on his sleeve, fishes around in his jacket pocket, looks down on me.

Pulling the blanket over my mouth to stifle a cough I ask, "You're going to Colorado?" I wonder why he'd not divulged this the night before. We'd skied there as kids and I wondered if my brother planned to shimmy back into a ski pants, lift-ticket persona again.

"No. Vale *Oregon*" he gives his chin a quick heft, like I should be able to hear the different pronunciations distinguishing acres of onions and a rocky mountain high.

"Before you go, can you go to town and get my prescription filled?"

A week before Christmas I'd gone to the county clinic in Mendocino to see about my cough and was prescribed Tetracycline. I hadn't filled the prescription which was still in my wallet. With my history of upper respiratory disease, at this stage, antibiotics were the surest cure around, yet a snow-bound mountainside away.

"Nope," is his reply. Not even a sorry, just, "Going to finish out a job in Vale."

Mark pulls two foil-wrapped packages from his pockets and leaves me with turkey and mashed potato leftovers as he lets himself out and more cold air in.

The next morning my throat and lungs feel like I'm gargling a mix of chainsaws and serrated bread knives. I knew if I didn't start taking antibiotics right away I'd likely take on the same position I'd found a deer in the summer before. Actually, it was a corpse by the time I came across it, tangled in a fence. Its neck was twisted in barbed wire, gouged and shredded; its snout was dried open in a scream stilled beyond any savior's hearing range.

Tetracycline would send me clear of that fence. But getting the prescription filled was about as easy a job as that deer had struggling to free itself from devil wire.

Hours after the next sunrise I hike down the mountain with an empty knapsack. I'm so sickly I have to rest against a pine, the bark patched with moss that's as green and clingy as the mucus I spit. The tree supports legs that want to collapse but the story of a hapless miner gives me the sheer will to push one foot in front of the other.

As the story went, the miner lived like a hermit, scouring tailings from boarded up shafts near Sumpter—once a nineteenth-century Oregon boom town, now famous for its summer flea markets. The hunters who discovered his skeletal remains concluded he died of exposure or other natural causes while hiking out for supplies one winter, as there was no evidence to support any malicious conjecture. The only identifying documentation discovered on him was a penciled shopping list in his breast pocket.

This happened a few years before I began building my own mountain hermitage. *Maybe his heart just gave out,* I think, willing my own to tick as I catch my breath. Or he lost heart; living alone in the woods too long can do that to a person. I know this as fact. I also know if I don't get moving, I'll end up like that man I named the shopping list miner; he deserved at least that eulogy.

If I let sickness straddle my stride I might freeze to death and then a hunter would find me, in or out of hunting season, clothing flapping like prayer flags over my stooped carcass. I would be referred to as "the dead girl" since I was young and my reasons for living alone didn't involve mining. But the prescription with my name on it and a driver's license in my wallet would void my anonymity. I do not want an *Yvonne the Dead Girl* story told so I hawk a loogie, put one boot down and force the other to follow even faster.

While the prescription is getting filled at Len's Drugstore I go to Chester's for groceries and buy a five-pound sack of oranges that nearly fills the knapsack of the same color. On the return drive I stop at the Nelsons, my closest full-time neighbors over three miles down the mountain.

Rhonda, the hazel-haired mother of this solid Mormon family, is the only one home. She invites me in and we exchange news. In the past, whether I've asked for help or not, she has been there for me. Once even manually jacking up a car with a flat tire in order to drive me to the hospital when I was sick with tick bite. With her sixth sense, her super-power mothering, she can see beyond my croaking sickness, past the hollow of my eyes a kinship lacking. Heartfully, she again includes me in her fold even though I am not blood family. She makes me stay until her son Matt, same age as me, returns so he can drive me all the way up to the cabin in their four-wheel truck, a prospect I accept. As we are leaving Rhonda says, with that little Mona Lisa smile and peaceful twinkle in her eye, "Lavon, are you going to join us for our New Year's Eve celebration at church?"

"When?" I ask.

"Why, December thirty-first, of course." Rhonda gives me a *What's the matter with you* look.

Of course, I knew when New Year's Eve was celebrated but I hadn't been tracking days so well since I took sick. I knew, though, I needed to be in Mendocino by New Year's Day because Leona said she'd be back by the second and ready to work. I also knew I was in no condition to drive hundreds of miles only to sleep in the back of what was responsible for my jousting with pneumonia.

I accept Rhonda's invitation to a church function, not the first one or the last one. Not so much out of desire for human connection but to atone for another invitation she'd once extended when I showed up at a wedding reception in the church's common area wearing a knee-length skirt, sketchbook in hand.

Over the next days I let the antibiotics kick in and try to figure out a proper outfit.

Five shiny, galvanized steel trash cans are lined in neat rows beneath the cabin. Each one acts as a kind of closet. Some contain a mix of my present and past apparel. Dresses, skirts, petticoats mix with wool shirs, work boots, and other frilly stuff that would snag in the forest.

Three days of eating oranges and drinking so much rosehip tea my pee blooms like roses in the snow, and sleeping in a cabin so warm I sweat, is time enough for the antibiotics to kick in. By New Year's Eve morning I feel well enough to rummage a wardrobe out of garbage cans.

Inside one, next to a pair of pitch-and-soot-tanned Raichle boots is the garter belt to hold up the nylon stockings I wore as an adolescent and pantyhose I later wore to work in inky offices with copy machines and self-correcting Selectric IBM's. Next to a Woolrich shirt with brush-fire burn holes is the yellow knit skirt suit, too prissy to wear to the office, worn reverently to Sunday mass instead. When I reach down to pull it out the hem snags on a garter snap, the other end hooking into the left eye of a Bass loafer.

Unraveling this jetsam wound together by a classy-dressed past, I spy, like a rock crab scared into hiding, a lonely bra. My figure hasn't changed since I last wore this clothing, but I am pretty sure, now accustomed to jeans and lumberjack shirts, I've outgrown anything intimately refining. Trying on a lady-like outfit like this again will surely send me kicking and bucking.

I hang the yellow skirt and jacket behind the stove, hoping the heat will release the wrinkles and not melt the egg-yolk-yellow synthetic fabric. The pantyhose is full of runs and tossed into the rag bin. The nylons are sound as the garter belt I recall wearing to church, the metal and rubber clips creating fleshy indentations in a bottom positioned upon hardwood pews.

Debilitated as I've been over the past days, I remain diligent about my hygiene. Bucket baths have sufficed, but I relish a sudsing beyond what I've been able to maneuver, perched like a gargoyle in the kitchen sink. Before I am ready to socialize I want a lengthy shampoo under a long and reliable hot shower and know where to find this luxury.

An hour before dusk it is dark enough to light a lamp. Instead, I turn down the wicks, fold the outfit squarely over the Bass flats, the right shoe stuffed with the garter belt, nylons, the left with a forlorn bra. These are placed in the knapsack atop few toiletries, an old sketchbook and a bottle of Tetracycline.

After checking in with the Nelson's, I drive to town and check into a hotel built from sandstone blocks. A comfort I haven't budgeted but figured

I deserved since surviving lung-eating disease and Christmas dinner with my brother. Plus, I didn't have the vigor to hike back in the dark to the cabin after the party. A room with a private bath is twelve dollars a night. Eight, if you share a shower down a hallway Norman Bates would feel right at home meandering.

The old man behind the registration desk has dandruff on his shoulders, slick as snow on the outside sidewalk. He says little beyond the price as I exchanged a ten and two ones for a brass key attached to a plastic fob big as a freshwater perch. I probably could have saved four bucks because I didn't see another soul in that hotel all night.

My room with a private bath is as cold as the cabin had been until I kindled a roaring fire. I rotated the steam heater knob to high, hoping it can muster comfort fast as a wood stove and turn on the television to keep me company. As the room warms I scrub and scour until I am sure the water heater is drained and Norman Bates will have to take a cold shower. The black and white TV screen undulates values of static as I fumble with garter and bra clasps less nimbly than the snow-tire chains I was am, by now, more adept at fastening.

By seven o'clock my long hair is dry and sheeny brushed and I am dressed in clothing foreign as the young woman who once so casually wore them. Cinched into lingerie, I identify with the Christmas-night horse's harness. Instead of bolting I shoulder my orange knapsack, lighter now with only pens, an old sketchbook and a wallet.

The LDS parking lot is solid with cars and trucks. I park beside a hay-littered flatbed and do not set the emergency brake, fearing that it will freeze stuck and impede a hasty retreat.

Standing in the doorway and scanning the congregation for my neighborly hosts, I instantly calculate my skirt is the shortest among the female equation. If anyone notices, they don't mention it. Instead, these Mormons, known to me or not, open their ranks to welcome me into this celebratory flock. Raised Catholic, I cannot recall enough about my religion and don't know enough about theirs to know whether ecclesiastical beliefs or my hemline will contort our cordial exchanges. But if the outfit I wore to another of their parties hasn't condemned me, I am confident my more prissified dress has not disqualified me from their acceptance.

"We'll have pancakes at ten," says Matt, taking my parka and handing me a cup of red punch sweet as his caring gesture. "You can set your pack down over there." He points to a metal chair.

One sip later, I set the cup alongside the sketchbook and a Rapidograph pen, aligning them beside a nondescript placemat—one setting among many others on tables surrounded by kids and adults shuffling plastic tokens across game boards. I'd outgrown Candy Land and Chutes and Ladders and didn't plan to stay long enough to win a game of Monopoly, so I made gesture drawings in the sketchbook started my first winter at the cabin. I wanted to show my early work to Leona and brought it to the party to fill the final few pages—and to keep me from getting antsy.

"Having a good time Lavon?" Rhonda asks as she takes the seat beside me.

I thought I was until she asked. But when I look around at all the sunny families, I struggle inside to be free of this place I got myself snared into just like the poor deer I'd seen the summer before. Sheer politeness holds me back like barbed wire.

I stay seated, making small talk with Rhonda and say "Thank you," when Matt holds out a plate of pancakes. There are two of them nearly as big as the plate and one ham slice, thick as the pancakes, all slicked together with syrup.

"Mind if I look?" Glen, Rhonda's husband wanders over and picks up my sketchbook as I finger plastic utensils. This is the same sketchbook I'd brought to that wedding reception at the church before and I had forgotten it included more than landscape studies.

"No. Go ahead," I reply forking into a first bite then blotting syrup from my wrist with a paper napkin. The great father of this Mormon family thumbs the pages, then stares at one too long. I lean in for a closer look and my face turns red as the cup of punch posted by my elbow.

"They're flowers. Wildflowers opening in the spring," I prattle out a white lie and grab the sketchbook before Glen pages to several other drawings I'd copied from Betty Dodson's *Liberating Masturbation: A Meditation on Self Love.*

To stymie any remote possibility of a discussion revolving around these drawings that actually resemble sprung vulvas and not spring violets, I take a big, big bite of oozing pancake. With a full mouth it would be impolite to chew and carry on a conversation about vaginal flora.

Aunt Jemima dribbles over my bottom lip as I gum a saccharine mash. That mouthful, like all the people around here, is just too sweet to swallow. I don't fit in here, just like I will never again ease into a world where nylon stockings and bras and being girly are part of the social fabric. I pardon myself from this welcoming table.

The engine turns over on the first try and I steer clear of the LDS parking lot. I could just keep driving past the county's sole stoplight. By sunrise I'd likely reach the redwoods. But just down the street, in a creepy hotel, I have a warm bed waiting. Tomorrow I would not.

6. The Art Center

Before Leona left for Los Angeles, she told me about a friend's Airstream where I could stay rent-free. Several days before leaving for Christmas I'd hiked down to this trailer. It was parked below the throat of a shadowy yawn parting second-growth redwoods. With snow-banked mountain passes and icy alkaline flats in my wake it is dusk by the time I arrive there. No sooner have I downshifted the Datsun through the coastal gloom filling that forest shaft than I am swiftly sucked into mud, miring the truck's belly.

I open the door and set foot in the same quagmire impenetrably cementing the front and rear tires. This mud is not displaced with all my wedging of sticks and branches under the wheels, leaving me undeniably and helplessly stuck-in-the-mud as daylight fades as fast as my vigor and perseverance. I spend the night curled inside a clammy camper shell, dreaming of a toasty cabin and dry clothes in a garbage can.

In the morning I lace up boots left on the bumper, which are as mucky and sopping as the forest I slog through. Trailing fog like a swamp thing I search for signs of life at the end of rural driveways leading to ramshackle houses that are built off the grid and without a permit—architecture I am familiar with.

As I wander, the inland coastal fog gets me coughing again. My hacking is the sole sign of life stirred in the haze haloing a walkabout I pray will end at any place with a telephone. By the time the sun cuts a rug in the mid-morning brume I am facing a mossy-roofed, double-wide trailer.

Behind a sliding glass door, a woman is posed in a half-twist warrior lunge. Her breasts, like sea anemone, droop down a rib cage narrow as a piling. My knocking upsets her yogi glory and she unwinds to answer the door.

She doesn't introduce herself or ask my name, or even question why I look like a mud pie. "Of course," she says, crossing her arms over her chest in an *I'm getting cold* pose and pointing to a wall phone. As I thumb the telephone book she returns to the cobra, or cat, or spider or whatever animal her twisted spine was channeling.

"I'll call you right back," I say softly to the man on the other end of the line. I don't want to disturb the woman's posturing to ask her address, so I walk down the driveway and memorize purple numbers painted on a chunk of driftwood, then redial and repeat numbers to the man I spoke with only minutes before; a man who said help was thirty or more minutes away.

I wait outside on a mildewed doorstep where the woman can see me in my drowned-possum pose and I can glimpse her behind the window. *Mussel cracked open at low tide*, is what I note in a position she holds long enough to get me blushing. By the time the tow arrives the lady is sitting cross-legged, fingers pinched together like rock-crab claws, and om-ing.

The tow truck driver didn't notice the naked yogi, or if he did he didn't let on as his engine idled before the sliding glass doors. He is a nice, clean-shaven older gentleman smelling like Old Spice and experienced in getting people out of jams. I get in his cab. He follows my directions then whistles between his teeth when he glimpses the mired Datsun.

After he pulls the truck free the gentleman tow truck driver suggests I follow him into Mendocino because he knows that after all that jerking and jarring, the front end will need realigning.

While a mechanic balanced and aligned, I explore, meandering down the sea bluff board walk until it ends at a headland. I hang a right, walking the same path I followed on a recent dark, foggy Christmas Eve. Instead of stopping to look at the Victorian homes I stand in front of a sign, "The Mendocino Art Center." The gentleman tow truck driver had told me—as we waited on the yoga lady's steps—that this is where I might find a nice apartment to rent if I decided not to tackle the muddy road to the trailer.

An office receptionist shows me the only available room. When I hand over a check for the first month's rent to this woman I am assuming is named Mary, for that is the name engraved on her desk plate, she adds in with the receipt that there is one scholarship available in the fine arts program at the center.

By evening the Datsun is all straightened out and my muddy jeans and boots slump in the corner of a one room apartment with shared kitchen and bath. It costs eighty dollars a month but is a bargain compared to what I'd been living in. Plus there is all the electric baseboard heat I need to dry out my lungs.

Leaning back on that single bed I started thinking about accidents, how maybe they happen for a good reason sometimes and I guess this latest one landed me on the right side of another catastrophe of my own making. Before my head hit the pillow that first night in Mendocino, I finished off the gorp stored in the glove box for emergencies. I was fed and warm. I was okay.

The next morning a toilet flushing, a shower streaming woke me. Civilized sounds as foreign as the four sterile, white walls boxing me in. Over the last few years I'd slept in a rat shack, tent, log cabin, mildewed trailer and clammy camper shell. Being confined by sterile angles was consoling only in the sense I didn't wake up breathing in fog.

Whoever had used the shared bathroom had left the adjoining apartment, prompting me to get up and discover a note taped to the closed door of my room. *Hi, I'm Judy. I'm in the Stevenson Studio.*

Outside I take my bearings. Marine air, the crashing sea a block away vibrating the loamy sandstone beneath my dry boots. Across from a cypress tree courtyard, a Stevenson Studio sign designates the door of one building. Behind windows twice as tall as me, students stand behind easels. I take this as an omen, like the day I discovered a baby bird perched on a branch beside the creek. Deep down I know I've found my spot.

From the doorway I piece together the name Mary had given to me, one I'd written on my sketchbook, with the only man visible in this studio—the man who vetted scholarship students. I waited until the class took a break then approach him and introduce myself.

Several students gather around as the instructor flips through the pages.

"Nice line work," he says scrutinizing ink drawings of landscapes or interpretations of wildflowers.

"Can I keep this until Thursday?" asks the instructor with the salt and pepper sort of beard, never once changing his uncompromising expression.

On Thursday I return to the Stevenson Studio and stand just inside the doorway as an older female instructor positions a naked man on a human-sized lazy Susan. Five students are situated behind sculpting pedestals posted around this man who is posed like The Thinker—fist to chin, elbow on knee.

I try not to stare at the model's flaccid penis but can't help it especially after one curly haired girl removes her sock and shoe and approaches the model.

"There," she chirps, "that's better," then stands back to scrutinize the genital propped up with her anklet. She returns to her pedestal, her face as flushed as the model who is working hard to stymie an erection.

"Your foreshortening is off." The instructor points to the barefoot student's sculpture. She continues around the studio, referring to the model then noting perspective problems in her student's sculptures. As they concentrate on clay modeling, I see the instructor who took my sketchbook walk by the window. When he sees me, he turns and walks away. His direction prompts my own retreat and I head toward the door, shouldering a load of disappointment that I hadn't been selected. As swiftly as he left the instructor returns with my sketchbook.

Framed by the doorway, the instructor in front of me, I am imagining his words of rejection before he has the opportunity to say "Congratulations."

I'd been granted a scholarship to study at The Mendocino Fine Art Center. The award meant I had to end my apprenticeship with Leona. If anthropomorphism extends to inanimate objects, then I am sure her little house breathed a sigh of relief as it watched me pack up my carpentry belt.

Life in the seaside village is predictably secure; plenty of warm electrified buildings are open to me. This Life of Riley prevails in simple rituals like flicking a switch for light or heat as opposed to lighting wicks, felling, bucking and splitting wood to stoke a fire. I didn't have to chain up a truck with an engine block I hoped hadn't frozen so I could drive twenty-six miles for groceries.

But months living alone made me skittish, unsure of myself around people. Like a habituated squirrel I'd learned to take my peanut and run, cautious of risks up the sleeve of an outstretched hand.

On the other hand, I wanted as much contact as I could get with my new teachers with last names like Bothwell, Stevenson and Maxwell. Like most of my art center instructors, these sages were trained and influenced by Yaddo, Bauhaus and famed art institutes. Miriam and Ray Rice were two of these teachers.

The Rices lived close to the Stevenson Studio where I spent nearly every night messing around with clay or paint. If I found myself in a creative pinch I walked across the street, knocked on their seaside-seasoned door and one or the other would stop what they were doing to help me out.

One night Miriam—the one who had repositioned The Thinker on my first day—threw a robe over her nightgown, clenched the lusterless chenille tight around her muffin body and together we walked through wispy February fog. I shivered beside her, my cotton shirt sleeves rolled above elbows, my hands caked in clay.

"It's the chin." Miriam circles the life-sized human head. She examines every angle of the clay piece anchored to a rotating stand, eyeing it like a doctor, conjuring up a diagnosis that won't upend the patient when delivered.

For the past week, from nine in the morning to noon, along with other students I'd been sculpting the head of a live female model and the project was to be ready for grading on Monday morning. It was Saturday night and even with finishing touches, I could see my bust failing. It was proportional and symmetrical. Yet, as much as I applied and cut away, her features were skewed.

"It's the chin," Miriam repeats and nods at the protuberance.

Plumbing a double angle scraper down the forehead and glancing between my face and the clay expression, Miriam concludes, "You put your chin on the model. It's tucked back like you hold yours. Like you are waiting to get socked."

More fiddling and a face-lift earns me a solid B.

On another night, demonstrating how to apply a mix of Damar Varnish and Dorland's Wax Medium to seal a dry oil painting, Miriam advised me to never learn to type. She reasoned that if I did it would lead to jobs that did not involve a paint brush, sculpting tools, pencil or pen. I didn't tell her I taught myself to type on a garage sale typewriter and that this hadn't led to any real work yet.

Ray Rice taught me how to wire and weld an armature to construct a cement playground sculpture I designed on paper. His creative expertise raised my expectations of masonry tools I'd used on more practical applications like footings and foundations.

From January through May I painted, drew and sculpted every day in buildings designed for these purposes only. I augmented my studies with physiology, color healing and anatomy textbooks—Barcsay's and Gray's—cross referencing and adding to what I learned in studios. Each month I painted the full moon over the Pacific Ocean where I learned to capture light reflected rather than absorbed like in the mountains I'd left in order to shore up my art education.

At the end of May I had to move out of my apartment for the tourist season, or else pay per week what I paid for a month's rent. This was fine by me. Classes were out until the fall. I had the cabin to live in until I returned to art school in September when rents were again student-friendly.

I knew I would need something beside myself and the wilderness to talk to through June, July and August. Days before leaving Mendocino I found a replacement.

"Pure Seal-point Siamese from a litter of five," claimed the woman sitting beside a cardboard box of kittens in front of the co-op. She was drinking fresh carrot juice from a wax-coated cup and her orange mustache reminded me of Halloween when she held that black mask fur ball next to her cheek and kissed it goodbye.

I named the kitten after a Lakota Indian word for sweat lodge, a place for purification. I also took the woman's word that it was male though it was still so young its bits hadn't dropped, it's sex a guess. It wouldn't have made a difference anyway. Inipi was not gender specific.

7. Break In

In late May, before returning to spend summer at the cabin I mailed a note to Dan Gray: *Please leave my truck in the meadow with the keys under the seat.* This Ford was my first truck, a beast of pistons, points and rods as problematic to steer as it was to upkeep. I named it Tank because it could tackle stretches of road sure to torque axels, puncture oil pans and crack mufflers of slighter chassis. It is the truck I use for hauling what the Datsun can't manage.

Dan Gray was an ex-logger, with a perpetual lopsy grin, gratis of a Doug fir kickback, a disfiguring accident pretty much concluding his full-time profession behind a chainsaw. Surgeons patched and pounded his cheeks, chin and nose back in place. Still, his face was wrecked. Like Tank, he was a lug of dents, and reliable most of the time. I'd known the man as long as I'd owned the truck.

Beyond those misaligned cheek bones, Dan was a genuine guy who sold used things to cobble together a living. Bargaining over a drawknife one summer is how I met him. The same day he convinced me to buy a second-hand beater. I repaid his courtesy by letting him drive Tank while I was away and he was supposed to leave it parked in the meadow before May rolled over to June.

Maybe he never checks his mail, I think as dust powders the little truck's eggshell-green paint job on the last stretch of road. On this blue bird day, before switching off the ignition and parking below the cabin I'm swearing at the sight before me.

Five-gallon plastic storage containers are upended below the porch steps, trounced and gashed open. Red wheat, mung beans, soybeans, white rice, long brown rice, corn, wheat groats, rye berries and powdered milk speckle the ground in pecks and mounds. A year's worth of food, that my Mormon neighbors had advised me on how to store, is mixed among lady slippers and tender yarrow stalks. Dozens of buckets of legumes and grains, two twenty-five-pound tins of honey and two containers of powdered milk are strewn about the hillside. I shuffle through the mess, scale the hand-hewn steps, and unlatch the door.

Inside, everything is exactly as I left it; the ivory-linen tablecloth-draped maple dinette is stationed beneath the window, the matching rocker is sitting before the wood stove, and the tamarack-pole ladder is leading into the loft. I open the windows, sweep out a few mouse turds, and unspool cobwebs from corners.

In the loft I make up a foam mattress bed with Tweety Bird sheets, faded as my copy of *The Prophet*, then haul buckets of water from the creek, split wood, trim kerosene lamp wicks and lay a fire. The rest of the afternoon finds me on the woody end of a pointy shovel and steel-fanged rake scoring grains and legumes into piles and replacing what is salvageable into holey containers, restocking them again beneath the cabin.

After a long day reclaiming food stores, unpacking the truck and stowing a summer's worth of supplies I am relaxing in front of the fire when commotion on the porch upends my respite. I'm not expecting company because it is well after sundown and everyone I know in these parts goes to bed after the sun sets in order to wake before it rises again. Unfolding myself from the rocker, I stand and stare out the window to see my open-mouthed reflection and a bear—the very first I've seen here—black as the night it retreats into.

Too scared to scream, to gasp or even to elicit "Oh shit," I back away, scale the ladder then pull it up rung by rung into the loft. I do not climb back down to blow out the lamps or even to pee outside—a necessity I accomplish inside a Mason jar emptied of pencils and pens.

In the morning, cracking open the door then cautiously stepping onto the porch, I bang the fire poker against a metal waste can until I am sure the coast is clear or deafened by my racket, then attend to the grain containers again ransacked from underneath the porch. By noon what is left of my re-salvaged stores are inside patched plastic tubs and I drive the little truck to town in search of its big brother.

"Hey." Dan Gray sees me under the cottonwood tree shading the curb where I am standing next to Tank. A broken smile on his face, this lopsided lumberjack lumbers across the lawn in front of his house to greet me.

Unfortunately, my big truck shares Dan Gray's expression of fate; it is in sorry looking shape. At some point after I handed him the keys he had rolled it. Surprisingly, that accident somewhat realigned the jammed driver-side door he had smashed in the summer before. Now it opens and mostly latches securely again.

"Tried to push it out," Dan nods to the roof. "Just caved too deep. Sorry about that."

He does not offer to pay to have it repaired. I lock the Datsun and hoist myself into the Ford. Later in the week I will hitch-hike to town and drive the elfin truck back to the mountain's lumbering feet.

"Keys are under the seat," Dan looks away forlornly as I slam Tank's door then slouch down to shift the clutch of my mammoth, mutilated truck with an empty tank.

At the post office I jot a postcard to Jim. "I'm back. Can you come up?"

More than someone I had hired to help me build my cabin Jim was my friend and mentor. I hoped he would find time this summer to help me shake the roof, a job that would take me all season without his muscled assistance.

Unless we made unannounced visits to each other's off-the-grid places we communicated through postage-stamped mail. The nearest phones to our clandestine mountain homes—he shared his with a wife and two kids—were screwed to cement walls or hung in glass-sided telephone booths over ten miles away.

Postcard sent, I climb into Tank and steer it to a gas station before heading to Prairie City to reconnect with other old friends.

"Lavon's back!" Anabell yells over her shoulder as she opens the kitchen screen door and pulls me in for a hug.

"Tell her ta' come in and have some supper," replies a voice as familiar to me as the stubble-chinned man seated at the faded Formica table.

I first met Del and Anabell Taynton when I was building the cabin. Every board foot of flooring, every rafter, nearly every stick of lumber in my cabin was cut and planed at Del's one-man lumber mill. As our business transactions increased so did our friendship. Like the Nelsons, my Mormon neighbors, the Taynton's offer non-judgmental support, care and concern I'd never known after the loss of my parents. They were also the first people to call me Lavon.

Anabell and Del were both in their sixties when I first met them, worn by the kind of roughhewn lifestyle that is fast to claim those effete of body and brain. They survived a depression and raised a good batch of kids; they knew their minds, how to mind their own business, how to live on and off the land without exploiting either province. To them I am a curiosity for choosing to live a rural lifestyle they had no option to sidestep.

"Was born workin'," Anabell said to me, more than once. Then detailed how all that "liftin' and haulin'" ruined her woman parts when she was young. Stories later retold in my own feminine makeup.

Because it is noon, an hour I've been conditioned to enjoy lunch, I accept their supper invitation.

Anabell sets down a bowl of stew dappled with potatoes and gray meat chunks. My first bite is a reminder of what I normally do not eat, but with these folks the karma is right.

Del butters bread with a knife he holds in a hand curved like a claw crafted by the line of work it took to cut off parts of a finger and thumb. Between bites we catch up. When my bowl is wiped clean I get right to the point.

"There was a bear at the cabin last night."

Del taps the Tupperware caddies filled with instant tea, coffee and sugar between our bowls as if to draw my attention. "About half a mile above that cabin you built, there's a cave. Bears hibernate in those rocky outcrops around it."

I've been inside the loamy mouth of this cave, ringed by rusted cans and old cooking pots shot full of holes. A miner, way, way before my time lived there. He was chiseling toward the gold vein that drew men to Canyon Mountain—the source of my creek and a place to pan out dreams.

My brother told me he once spent a night inside this cave. I didn't believe him until poking about one afternoon my flashlight spotted an empty Jack Daniels bottle slick with bat shit.

At supper that afternoon I tell Del I was not aware the area around the cave was a haven for bears. Nor was I aware that later down the line I'd be the one to eventually keep its grave heart beating.

Del tells me to watch for ripped up stumps and windfalls, signs the bears are nosing about. I'd noticed these on a hike the day before but thought nothing of it. Now I see the connection and imagine myself splayed out in strips and chunks instead of wood pulp.

"You gotta a gun?" Anabell asks, lighting the cigarette that signals she is through with her stew.

I shake my head.

48

My experience with weapons was limited to a child's Daisy BB air rifle and a slingshot, targeting empty soup cans and tree trunks. I wanted to keep my sights on this.

Anabell takes my empty dish to the sink, turns and says, "If ya don't have a gun then ya better get you a dog for protection."

I wondered if a cat would do.

8. Settling In

The first years on the mountain I had no time to be introspective or to think beyond building the cabin and learning to live in the wilds I was settling inside and outside of myself. Just keeping warm and fed kept me from thinking about a sore-filled past. I began healing by working myself to the bone—over two hundred of them bagged inside a hide of curing adolescence.

Besides, introspection was an occupation for people with time on their hands—soft-spined people curved into over-stuffed leather chairs who mused upon their fancied, gilded, tortured, or milquetoast lives. People who leisured in the moment, to read between the lines, to reconcile with, or time out cognitions. Self-absorbed people who didn't have to think about where or how they got their water or heat.

At this point I wasn't one of *those people*. Simply keeping myself warm and fed kept me too occupied to repercuss upon the dowry of misery that indirectly led me to Oregon.

I was more like a pampered version of *those other people* who plotted fate on the Oregon Trail over a century and a half before. People who wore dusty, sweat-stained buckram bonnets and buckskin britches, who hitched their futures to oxen carts before this land was even named the thirty-third state.

Compared to those pioneers my route was breezily-paced, compliments of a Rand McNally road atlas, four cylinders and four tires speedily traversing smooth-linking asphalt. This groomed passage was much shorter too. The original 1800's, 2100-mile trail beginning in Missouri began for me in Minnesota. Gas stations and a reliable car enabled me to cover in minutes the same distance it took animal-drawn caravans to cover in a day.

Though my direction was surely mapped, I encountered forks in the road and Meek decisions and like those pioneers I knew what it was to lose loved ones along the journey. But, crying about loss was a luxury I couldn't afford. *Woe is me* tears would only hold me back.

Now, secure in this log home with a door held fast, I could spare time to stew on leftovers simmering on my psyche's back burner. Yet, I was as reluctant to trail these memories as I was to explore a shadowy cave—both unsettling prospects made me want to drink Jack Daniels to forget.

I missed my parents and the sanctuary of a family to fall back on when things got out of hand and I failed to stay on the right side of myself. But thinking about the past messed with my present relationship with the wilderness—a monogamous affair until bears turned it into a ménage a' trois.

Encountering a bear my first night back was a portent of what keyed that summer on the mountain. Rationalizing to myself that black, brown and cinnamon bruins roamed these ranges for generations didn't reconcile our immediate co-existence.

Every night now, sleep is timed-out by thumping and bumping sounds on or under the porch. This commotion keeps me awake in the loft until dawn when I rise to deal with what has stolen my slumber. In the morning I straighten grain tubs dragged out again from underneath the cabin and rake the spoils, either dumping them down the outhouse or burying them until there is nothing left. It would take too long to dig a pit deep enough to cover two pulverized five-gallon honey tins clawed open, the screw tops chewed off. These remain roped to a distant bull pine.

Before dark I haul enough water and wood inside so I don't need to go outside until well after the first morning light. I replace the Mason jar and rely on an empty coffee can, purposely not drinking anything after sunset. Each night before retiring I read before the fire, a forged rebar fire poker, for protection, within reach. The solid log walls muffle the whoosh of the rising creek. In this silence truths have time to speak and I have no choice but to listen.

By the time I've managed to hear myself clearly, the fire has condensed to tomato-soup-colored embers and I damp it with a wet log hoping the smoke will repel nighttime visitors. In the loft I bed down beside the fire poker, only to wake a couple hours later to familiar clamor.

Before I can say, "Come on baby show me what you're made of," I must throw off bed covers and feel for a match to light a lamp to find the metal trash can in order to bang it with the poker. The tinny resounding scares off the dream wrecking intruder. Back under cover, I hold hands with metal rigid as my body, my molars gnashing steely qualm. Over a week's worth of these nightly charades erodes my pearly enamel and carves bruising crescents under my sleep-deprived eyes.

"You damn thing!"

Jim hoists me up in a great bear hug.

"You look like you haven't slept in a week."

Besides being right on time, 8 a.m., Jim's also correct in his observation as I greet him beside his truck parked below the cabin.

After Jim releases me from a welcoming grip, we catch up on his family. He hoists his tool box out of the truck bed. Hand-built out of two-by-eights the kit is nearly as heavy as the tools inside it.

Even though he has raised his rate from when he helped me build the cabin, what I pay Jim now is an invaluable reminder of my worthlessness in worlds of the heavy hauling and lifting necessary for structural building. He has muscles and carpentry skills that will forever remain undeveloped in me. Over six feet tall, Jim is chiseled physique, his biceps thick as my thighs. In another era Michelangelo would have hired him as a model and Florence would be famous for Jim not David.

Jim is on the pedestal of the men I respect the most. I hire him to do the work I cannot do or even imagine doing alone and would pay him ten times more if I could afford to. Even then, this sum would not cover his friendship, which is priceless.

After a little catching up—Jim's wife and kids are fine—I tell him about my mangled truck, the bear, then we get to work. Still early morning, it is warm enough to wear only a t-shirt and Jim and I settle into working together like we've never lost a beat.

He demonstrates how to lash a slip knot around a bolt of tamarack shakes then climbs onto the roof and tosses one end of the coiled rope down. I lash each splintery square he jigs up and over the eave. When there are six bolts on the roof, I crawl out the loft window and get to work. Pounding in sixteen-penny nails we shake to the peak then call it quits for the day. Three bales balance below the pitch waiting for me to nail them into the north face.

"Get some sleep tonight," Jim says as he reorganizes his gear in the sturdy-as-a-house toolbox.

"Only if the bear sleeps too." I unbuckle my leather tool belt and lay it on the bottom step.

"I'm thinking about getting a gun." Nails spill out of the pouch and I bend to pick them up. "What do you think?"

"You damn thing," Jim hoists his kit, bent at the waist by the weight and looks down on me as I scrounge sixteen-pennys. "That bear won't bother you if you don't bother it," advises my sage, mentor, and friend.

For the first time since I have known Jim, his advice will prove dead wrong.

9.Crossing Hairs

"Schreeeeeee! Schreeeeeee! Schreeeeeee!"

"Shit! Shit! Get!" I scream back and fend off a swooping bird with talons aimed at my scalp. It circles tighter, targeting, I figure, the smaller prey protectively picked up and pulled fast to my chest. But its bull's-eye appears to be my skull rather than the feline snug between my breasts.

"Sorry little buddy." I drop Inipi in a poof of road dust and grab a nearby evergreen branch.

Brandishing it like a Samurai warrior, twirling like a fan dancer on amphetamines, I make some intimidating moves myself. As I fend off arid advances, my hair feathers in breezy wisps whipped up by wings that bank sharply then fold against a downy bosom heaving atop a raggedy fir crown perch. I've no idea how long it takes eggs to hatch or for fledglings to fly but after that first encounter, I wear a small aluminum pail on my head whenever I walk by that goshawk nest.

Like the bear, goshawks were never a problem up here before. Now that I've finished the cabin—all the chainsaw growling, pounding and swearing quieted in wall logs—the woodland creatures must feel safe to come out again. Rattled from that close encounter of a winged kind, I dust off my cat and finish gathering roadside tinder then prepare to spend the morning drawing in the loft.

I should have been on the roof nailing down tamarack shakes, but instead I was cleaning new Rapidograph pen nibs, 0000, 000, 01, 1 and 2, purchased in Eugene. Ammonia and water, I'd discovered, did as good cleaning those pin-head-sized points as did pricey solvents sold in stream-line jars architects favored.

While preparing to exercise those points, I was also counting carpenter ants climbing in and out of a freshly burrowed hole in the dormer loft windowsill supporting Red Wing mugs and Mason jars filled with brushes, pencils and pens. When the nibs were nested into ink-filled cartridges I sat down to draw the forest on the other side of the window, my concentration broken by the ants streaming up, over and down the windowsill framing my composition.

There are six tubes of silicone wrapped in pink fiberglass insulation under the cabin. They'd not frozen over winter and I glide one into the caulking gun then shoot a plug into the carpenter ant hole in progress. This immediately stems the army and any deserters are squished with a matchbook advertising a mail-in drawing contest awarding $1,000 to the winner.

The tube is still nearly full so I draw a wobbly bead between the sill and window for extra weather stripping. Intently caulking away, with a birds-eye view of the creek I assume the dark gap on the other side of the bank is just another hole in the foliage, until it moves.

A muscled bundle of black fur bumbles through the brush and noses the refrigerator box I built from two-by scraps and sunk with boulders in the creek. It claws apart boards with tea-saucer-sized paws, snags a head of iceberg lettuce and toys it to shreds, then spears a chunk of Tillamook cheese. When it's done, the black bear walks back into the bush with a bread bag in its mouth.

By then the caulking gun, still squeezed tight in my grip, is as empty as my refrigerator. The matchbook—really tricking wannabe artists to buy a mail-in drawing course—is plastered under a gooey silicone mess.

The next day, while on the roof banging down shakes, I spy a bear trundling up the path, perhaps sniffing out buried grains or a Tampax dropped into the privy pit. Rather than being scared away by all my hammering, it merely stretches its ebony neck, snorts, snout twitching and heads uphill. From that day on I burn all waste and pack into town any garbage I cannot set aflame.

"Dan do you have a gun I can borrow to shoot a bear?"

In the time I'd known Dan Gray, king of second-hand sales and questionable bargains, I'd only bought things from him. Borrowing was a new kind of transaction with a similar ring. "Only have a shotgun." He rubs a phantom cheek bone. "Might be able to kill em' if ya' get the barrel real, real close to his ear." He scratches his corrugated neck. "Or maybe his eye."

Dan goes inside his house while I wait in the back yard among contraptions in all states of disrepair and tools in all degrees of dereliction are positioned haphazardly on plywood sheets supported by sawhorses. Mostly Dan sells things as-is and won't cut bargaining slack even if a tool is broken. "Easy ta fix it, and steel's better than anything new," he rationalizes before sealing a deal. I've bought a drawknife, ax, posthole digger, hammer, hand saw and various other tools which have to be pounded out, sharpened and oiled to work. Every time I go to his backyard, I walk back out with some tool he has convinced me to purchase because he says "It will come in handy someday." He even convinced me to buy a busted truck and it wasn't his to sell.

He returns and shoves a rusty planer and dead chainsaw to the side of a table, lays down and, unzips a mildewy shotgun case.

"Here." He hands me the gun inside.

My arms sag with an alien weight I strain to level but instead settle the rifle butt on my foot and look down the barrel.

"Hey!" Dan shoves the firearm away from my prying eye.

"I just wanted to see if there was a bullet inside."

He grabs the gun from my limp wrist clutch and raises the stock to his hulking shoulder, shuffles into a wide stance, "Look down it, not in it," he says turning toward me before aligning his sight down the steely blue shaft.

"You point that little piece of metal stickin' straight up at the end at what ya want to hit. And boom!" He recoils from an imaginary shot.

That very evening on the porch, while reading Leonard Cohen's musings on the upturned breasts of fallen sparrows, the opportunity to draw a bead arose.

Concluding I am not seeing double, I lay down the volume and lift the rifle lying inert beside three open poetry books, stand, spread my legs and level the barrel. Aim the piece of metal stickin' straight up at one bear, the larger one with a gray muzzle. It is beefier and more vexing than the sleeker smaller bear standing beside it, that looks like the one who ripped apart my refrigerator box.

Rushing adrenalin unsteadies the bead I struggle to fix on some portion of that bear as it noses out that same box nailed back together—nothing now but scent inside. When the cross hairs steady over a square of undu-lating hide, I slowly squeeze the trigger like Dan Gray had only so recently instructed.

The barrel bounces up as the butt and live shell drop, the cartridge roll-ing to rest in a floorboard crack. With half a rifle in hand and of no use at all, I resort to the big guns—bang together the wastebasket and fire poker.

10. Me, Myself and I

Emery swipes his hands down a greasy bib apron as I settle on a round red swivel stool at the end of the counter. I give a little wave not to let him know I'm ready to order but to remind this cantankerous acquaintance that I am back. He walks toward the cash register on my right but instead of ringing up a sale he leans over the counter, pinches his lower stubbled lip and mumbles "Look what the cat's drug in."

I smile and order the usual. "Two fritters and coffee. Please."

"Want cream and sugar?"

"Yes, please." Normally I drink my coffee black. At Emery's Bakery Café I do not: his brew the color of the John Day River and as tasty too.

I first met Emery when the idea of building a log cabin was still that. A pie-in-the-sky dream an eighteen-year-old girl punctured with a bow saw gone wild. Back then, green as the tree that nearly creamed this feller's first attempt, I nursed a headache in this come-at-able café named after the man who ran it.

Emery is as baldpated and blistery as he was the first time I met him. Somehow I got past the gruff demeanor that kept some people away and others in line in his business. Mostly I stopped in more hungry for a chat than something to eat. Usually he spared a minute for me between slinging food-filled plates to customers. Today I've come with a single question.

"Can I use your dumpster?"

This question leads to discussion of the spoils in my truck bed and Emery quietly listens before serving plated fritters.

"Ya got a gun?" he asks, turning his back to get the coffee pot then moving down the counter filling or topping up cups. He doesn't hear me when I answer. "I did. But it broke the first time I fired it."

As he is ringing up my tab, Emery says, "Ya know I was just readin' in the paper the other day about this couple in Alaska. They was being bothered by a grizzly. So, the fella he tells his wife ta go up on the roof and stay there and he goes fer help."

I wait for my change and roll out a toothpick from a dispenser next to a bowl of matchbooks by the cash register.

"When he came back she'd been eaten alive. Parts of her strewn over the roof."

"Oh. Dumpster's out back," Emery hands back change as he points past the kitchen.

That night, I sit in the rocker reading about what Leonard Cohen has to say about hunters kneeling before a woman's hem…

Even in her sleep
She turns away from them…

My attention twitches between stanzas; every branch snap, breeze whistle, creek-rock rumble keying me tighter with terror I cannot placate. Different to the free-falling fear I knew growing up without the security of a home to cushion a hard landing, this dread is stoked as I imagine being shredded like the honey cans in Emery's dumpster or like the lady on that rooftop in Alaska.

The noise under the porch, agitating my reading, is not stirred by breeze. It is the maladroit sounding of something large and moving beneath the floorboards. I strain to imagine it is an eloquent poet rehearsing inspirational verse, and not a dumb bear. Wiser from experience I rise and jump up and down, crashing pots and pans together. This primitively choreographed impromptu, known through eons as the *Scared Enough to Pee Your Pants Dance*, does the trick. The illiterate intruder is frightened away and I resume my reading about dreading a time…

when your mouth
begins to call me hunter…

But I can't stop from thinking, *I've got to kill a bear before a bear kills me.*

I bookmark *The Spice-box of Earth*, pull out a sketch pad and start drawing as an alternative to plotting murder.

In the morning it is pouring. Rain pools in bear tracks I discover and confirm by cross referencing *Reader's Digest North American Wildlife.* Their muddy calling cards on the porch and window sill advertise a noisy nocturnal visit I'd slept through because of roof-drubbing rain. It is a visit clearly imprinted by three sets of tracks stamped about the cabin's perimeter.

The unwavering deluge outside prolongs my time inside. Dry and content under a solid roof, I drink cup after cup of Taster's Choice instant coffee, reviewing and revising drawings of the night before.

One entire sketchbook page is filled with unstable perspective lines. Drawn without a ruler and by kerosene lamplight, these architectural renderings are lopsy instead of arrowed- level. Aided by daylight, an eraser and twelve-inch stainless steel straightedge, these re-drawn lines lead to respective vanishing points concluding in a Rapidograph-penned bear-proof cellar. After a fourth cup of coffee I've decided to top it off with a log studio.

On the rare occasion I have, a human visitor here, the cabin feels congested even with the addition of only one other body. Surrounded by thousands of wilderness acres, this twenty-by-twenty-four-foot space can really only comfortably accommodate three if they are limited to…me, myself and I.

If I had extra space like a studio, I wouldn't need to set my easel on the porch to paint. A separate studio would also free up more room in the cabin to entertain a guest. But figuring how to design an effective bear-proof cellar studio is as likely as comfortably sharing the cabin. I sharpen another pencil.

By the time I'm filled up with coffee the sky runs like an open faucet and my limited architectural understanding has run its course. For over an hour I rework my drawings to include large windows on three sides and skylights above a porch as long as the fourteen-by-fourteen-foot floor plan. I choose these dimensions because they represent logs I figured I might maneuver alone. Then I'd only need help pouring a cement cellar, laying up the rafters, maybe roofing. All the rest of this second round in log-cabin building I plan to do relying solely upon me, myself, and I.

By early afternoon, the rain absorbs into a spongy sky. I use the break to pound nail holes in the bottoms of two empty green-bean cans, thread them with twine and tie both around my waist where with every step they conduct a clang-clang symphony hopefully in the key of a bear-scaring cacophony.

Tinkering down the muddy road, fire poker in hand, sketchbook in the other, I stop at the abandoned campsite where I once lived in a tiny green nylon tent while building the cabin. Kicking away reminiscence and duff, I hunker down on my haunches and measure my faint shadow. The hillside is heavily treed. Cutting the surrounding pine and fir would widen this woody aperture so full morning and afternoon light would flood this old haunt and the fallen could be bucked and skinned into building logs.

Hunched under dripping boughs, I realize the idea of erecting a studio—bear-proof or not—is just plain premature. There are too many tasks to finish at the cabin—shake the roof, carve bookshelves, board up the understory to keep out big animals, ditch water bars. Pack rats are another chore. Add to this list all the work required to simply live here. Building anything more means only more burden.

By early afternoon the rain stops and it seems a better way to spend this solstice afternoon is to run, au naturale around freshly-washed mountainsides. But my sense of duty prevails. I dress in going-to-town clothes—clean cutoffs and flannel shirt—then set out, on this first day of summer, to buy a load of one-by to board up the bottom of the cabin.

Sure as spring turns over into summer, Tank refuses to turn over. Usually I remedy this motorized incompliance by ratcheting out the plugs, scraping away crud, then using pilers to bop both the plugs and the battery terminals on their heads. This doesn't work today. I need a jump-start and the only engine around is inside a chainsaw casing, plain useless in travail linked to a piston engine. I put a pail on my head and start walking.

My idea is to borrow jumper cables from the Nelsons—my closest neighbors, three miles away—then drive back up in the Datsun, connect both truck terminals and hope Tank will turn over. I'd only observed a jump-start performed before and had to trust my mental retention would spark results. I hoped my neighbors were home and in a lending mood.

Safely past the goshawk dive-bombing range, I ditch the pail. No longer a bucket head, my ears tune to an engine whining somewhere over the wooded ridge and it is not under the hood of any type of vehicle negotiating Shit and Slide. It is emanating from a greasy crankcase belly inside a red tractor I see chugging around the judge's meadow.

The judge was really my closest neighbor a mile down. But he worked the circuit Monday through Friday and only came up to his cabin, situated above a grassy meadow, on long weekends. Right now, he would be convening in some musty county courthouse. Plus, he didn't even own a tractor so whoever was shifting around on that John Deere scaring up magpies must be a robber.

I'd heard about tractor-driving thieves and that these back-country burglars prized wood stoves and pirated them away in front-loader buckets. The judge heated with propane. So, the perp on the tractor either hadn't cased the place or had other loot in mind.

To stand by and witness larceny in broad daylight would not be in keeping with good neighborly conduct. Defenseless—I left the fire poker at the cabin—I charge down a slippery grassy slope to defend my neighbor's property with words.

"Hey! Hey!" I wave my arms until the driver catches sight of me and idles down.

Close enough to smell diesel, I take in the congenial, leathery face of the driver and realize he is Don Paulsen, a roly-poly, jolly, tobacco-chewing, jack-of-all-trades, who lives in the modern ranch-style house I pass by on my going-to-town drives. He is cutting the judge's high grass in return for the hay, he explains. Then I explain why I am out walking and he is as quick to oblige his own truck to jump-start Tank.

My ankles grip the hitch and I hold on to the tractor seat as we shake, rattle and roll down two miles of wet gravel road evaporating as the sun inches higher. Don idles down in the drive of his house and pulls up alongside the barn and we get into his big old red Ford and drive back to my cabin. After listening to a lot of Don's stories that seem to go on forever, my truck is jumped. Before leaving Don extends the first of many friendly overtures. "Come on down for a piece of peach pie," says this big-hearted rancher with magnanimity enough to range beyond his beloved livestock.

On the way down, a dirty, vanilla-colored horse with a head hefty as my truck grill blocks the rose-hip-guarded gate. I've seen deer and elk but never a horse up here before. Its shoed hooves imply this is not a wild ungulate but rather a groomed mount and it does not shy easily. Leaving the engine idling, I wedge rocks under the front tires, get out and yell "Shoo, shoo, get, get," until the horse sidles up slope, allowing me passage through the barbed wire gate that I latch closed in my wake.

I've accepted Don's invitation and stop at his house on the way to town. His wife, Orinda, doesn't seem as benevolent as her husband. When she opens the door it seems as if it's hard for her to even slice me a smile after she invites me "ta sit down" at the oval dining room table. Orinda is the antithesis of Don's physique and demeanor. String-bean thin, with an attitude sharp as her cheekbones. Still, she welcomes me, "for pie."

"Big or small?" She crosses her stick arms across a board chest, looks at the two plates colored like wood-duck eggs.

"Small please." She returns to the table, placing a plate with the biggest, juiciest slice in front of me, then a plate with a smaller portion in front of Don.

I center the serving before me on a white, Chantilly lace tablecloth that would appear just as fitting on the body of a blushing bride. Everything in the house is virginal fresh, neat as a pin, spic-and-span. Starched, crocheted coverlets drape two rocking chairs and one long couch. Framed pictures of weathered barns and perky sunflowers in rusty milk cans hang perfectly aligned on paneled walls. The house is air-conditioned and so clean a housefly would certainly die barren trying to find a breeding surface here.

Orinda in her crisp, pale-yellow blouse and matching slacks leans against a kitchen counter sterile enough to perform surgeries on and watches as I fork into flaky crust. Compared to her, I look like something scraped from barnyard boots.

"Take your hat off at the table." Don obeys his wife's command like he is programmed to. Brim in hand, he walks toward the pantry and places it atop a chest freezer.

On his way back to the table he asks, "Want some goat's milk with yer pie? Fresh this morning. Real cold by now."

Without waiting for a reply, he opens the refrigerator door and retrieves a Folgers Coffee can and pours out two glasses, then carries both to the table and hands me one. "Orinda don't much care for it," he says taking a slurp and sliding me a wink.

We eat sweet pie and drink gamey milk, make small talk and Orinda seems to warm to me until Don asks, "Want to see my turd collection?"

As with the goat's milk, Don moves before I can answer and swiftly returns to the table with a flat cardboard box that looks like it should hold a sharply-folded Brooks Brothers dress shirt instead of what's inside. He lifts the lid, unfolds tissue paper and spreads it beside his empty pie plate. Don pulls out and aligns the contents one by one, examining each piece of excrement as precisely as a diamond jeweler with a loop.

"This one's coyote. Ya can tell by the little bones in it. See?"

I do see; pin-sized phalanges claw out of fur-pricked, desiccated-fecal fissures.

"This here's elk in the spring, cause it's more like a patty." He holds out a furless, crumbly, cookie-shaped specimen.

"And this here's elk in the fall cause there's less fresh grass to eat." Don jiggles nuggets in his hand like dice.

"This is bear." He places an elongated excretion beside the elk patties. "Ya can tell because there's bark and ants mixed in with it, too."

All this time Orinda has her back turned, re-washing the empty pie pan. I'm engrossed in my first scatology lesson which ends abruptly when Don adds, after displaying a cougar poop, "Want ta see its thang?"

He ignores his wife's protest, reaches into his pocket and pulls out a small, ivory-colored awl.

"See how it's got this little curve at the end. Cougar's only animal I know with a bone in its thang."

Like many of the stories Don will tell me—stories with just enough credibility to make the outlandish sound convincing—I am left to contemplate the hillbilly toothpick he repockets.

"Thank you for the pie. I don't believe I ever had peach pie before," I say edgily, hoping to deflect the tongue lashing I sense Orinda is about to unleash on her husband. I carry my plate, recently scraped clean of a second piece, to the sink.

Orinda yanks it from my hand. "Wasn't good as fresh. These were canned," she says, scrubbing the plate with foamy vengeance. Can't get fresh peaches from Kimberly until July."

This is the most talkative Orinda has been since I arrived and I want to prolong the conversation and ask how to find this peachy philanthropist named Kimberly, but I'm eager to get to town to buy boards.

By now it's afternoon. Besides peach pie and goat milk, Taster's Choice has barely softened my hunger. I'm ragged from lack of sleep and my fingernails are jam-packed with engine grease.

"Do you really want to be doing this?" I question my haggard reflection in the rearview mirror and shift into gear.

"No!" I answer without hesitation.

"Is this the life you want to be living?"

"Hell no!" I am quicker to answer, popping into second.

I do not want to be on a mountainside ruled by bears and bossy birds. Then again, I *do* want to be on this mountainside and therefore these inconveniences must be brushed off as minor because, truthfully, this is the only place I have to call home.

Del is in the saw shed peaving a log on the line. Scab slabs topple onto a chain conveyor belt that drops them in turn onto a haphazard pile below the deck. The trimmings later transpire into spiraling smoke inside a teepee burner.

When Del sees me waving he switches off the gyrating saw blade tall as a man, and it whirs to a slow, ear-piercing stop.

"Hi Lavon." He removes his cruddy cap and wipes away sweaty sawdust.

Not one for small talk which is a big factor in business transactions around here, I get right to the point. "I need some one-by."

"What for?" he wipes his brow with a red bandana as seasoned as the cap he replaces on this thinning pate.

"I want to board in the bottom of the cabin."

"Cause of the bear?"

"Yep." I am learning the workings of one word that cuts the chase of small talk.

Del leads me to stacks of rough cut. Together we lift eight- and twelve-foot-long boards separated by sticker stock and load them into my truck bed.

"Lavon, don't go bustin' yer' milks," Del looks at the tank top beneath my flannel as I labor with a burden of four boards. I lighten the teat-popping load by two as I mull over this country colloquialism and button up my shirt before lifting anything more. On the last load I remove the red bandana in my back pocket and Stanley-staple it to the end of one twelve-footer.

I pay cash for the boards and drive to the shadowy side of the stone-walled Prairie City hardware store. There I buy a box of twelve-penny nails. I won't use all fifty pounds hammering the batting but it's half the price to buy nails in bulk than in a measured brown paper sack.

"Ya want a hand with that?"

"Oh thanks, I can do it myself," I tell the cashier.

He is the same man who told me the last time I was there, buying spikes, that being okay meant simply being warm and fed.

I crouch down to lift the carton, hoist it hip level and waddle out the door to remind him I am beyond okay.

With a huff and heave I drop the box and let it slide down boards angling over the tailgate. It thuds to a rest against the cab, the weight anchoring the boards to keep them from bouncing out—a strategy I wished I'd enacted the last time I hauled up a load of flooring.

The strange horse is back at the rose-hip gate and only swishes its tail when I beep. Doesn't move a muscle even after I lean on the horn and slam the door, twice for an effect that doesn't register a blink of its eye. It stands there like it owns the road; and it does, too, because I can't drive around a flank fat as the ingress is wide.

I get out, block the tires and pull the red rag board from the bed, swinging it overhead and hollering up a storm enough to scare a goshawk into outer space. Not that horse though. It remains grounded on hubcap-size hooves as its penis descends—confirming this is no mare—and pees a stream strong enough to erode the ground beneath its barrel chest. Drained, the horse clomps up slope allowing me to pass.

That night I collapse into a sleep broken by sounds I want to pass off as mice. In the morning I discover it wasn't rodents keeping me awake.

Since the bears ripped apart the creek refrigerator box, I must buy ice to keep perishables in the aluminum Coleman cooler on the porch. When I open the cabin door I see it is tipped over and three cracked eggs ooze next to an untouched block of Tillamook Sharp Cheddar, all in a melting puddle. A tomato and banana are mashed on the steps.

I build a fire with green twigs, hoping the smoke will scare away whatever is behind this trashing, then scrape up the runny eggs and fruit and dump the pulp down the outhouse. Right after sunset I carry the fire poker and an empty coffee can into the loft and pull up the ladder behind me. Intermittent racket on the porch keeps me awake until darkness leaks into dawn.

At sunrise I declare, "Today I am getting a gun."

11. Setting the Stage

"Why ya little fart!" Don Paulsen snorts as the rifle reports, slamming my back into his chest hard enough his hat tilts back.

"Blewed it clean apart," he says behind a grin nearly brown as the brim he repositions over his frosted pate.

A brassy energy stings through me like electricity. I'm still shocked by the kickback and the realization that I've drawn a bullseye the first time I fired a gun that didn't break in half. Despite a recoil enough to blow me over, I remained upright, with Don behind me, supporting my elbows.

"Try er' again." Don walks about 200 feet into the pasture and places another log on the stump, within range of the kitchen window where Orinda can see us.

I spread my legs again, level the barrel on the fence rail and center the sight on deadwood.

"Move back please," I tell Don, before pulling the trigger. Instead of a dead hit the log is winged, pivots and plummets.

Don zips the thirty-thirty into a scuffed scabbard and hands it back with advice.

"Can't really kill a bear with this unless ya' get real close to a vital spot like an eye or heart. But yer' a good shot."

This is the second time in a week a man has lent me a gun not powerful enough to kill a bear I aim to. Earlier that day I'd gone to Dan's to return his rifle. "Butt fell off," I say, handing back the stock and barrel separately.

"Never happened to me before," he replies shifting gun parts in each massive mitt.

That evening the sturdy thirty-thirty leans against the door jamb within reach of the rocker where I sit with a lonesomeness that plans to stay the night. Inipi sprawled limply across my lap doesn't move a whisker when I reach for a pen and notebook, turn up the lamp wick and begin to write.

I wonder if my need for aloneness is really essential to the development of myself or just the perseverance of some ego trip? Sometimes I lose sight of myself through these illusions that other illusions form that keep me from myself and others. I maintain this aura of individualism by cultivating a tight ring of solitude around me. But I think this stoic individualist stance can be blasted apart by my turn of heart for another. Love shatters my myth of an independent self. I know myself very well, but do not know myself in relation to others.

Love, my ass!

The bare truth is I am more familiar holding an ax, hammer or chainsaw than the hand of a lover. I can also handle a rifle more securely than a relationship because as of this day I have experience with a weapon.

My grasp on intimacy is as gaping as the crack over my bed. Between bears bungling about the cabin and the scritch-scratch and scrambling about in that space between the ceiling paneling, sleep when it comes to me is broken. I don't know if it's mice or pack rats making hay in the rafters but I figure the latter because of a lingering and perspicuous uric stench particular to those pom-pom-tailed rodents.

The bears have no taste for sacks of cement and lime stored under the cabin. These are good as last used. So are the two boxes of bait stored inside a metal Superman lunch pail. One box is for Kills Mice. The other for Kills Rats. When I leave the cabin for any length, I combine the two in an aluminum pie pan and set this strychnine stew under the sink.

In the morning, I mix and haul up a bucket of mortar into the loft along with chicken-wire strips and two fresh boxes of d-Con. I tear open each box and push them as far as possible into the ceiling paneling then staple galvanized wire over the gap and slather mortar over the mesh. The sloppy chink naturally defies gravity and plops out onto my head, repeatedly.

In art history I learned the Parthian Arch collapsed several times during construction. I recall this lesson, add in persistence and more mortar until the crack is sealed, then stick my head in the creek to wash away what I learned.

Not yet at its pinnacle to signal lunchtime, late morning sun already bakes down upon the cabin roof, signaling a hot day ahead. In a recent note to Jim I asked him to help me with the bear-proof studio plans. We are standing by the sink as he looks at my drawings. He asks questions and makes suggestions, then makes a declarative observation.

"Something smells dead," he says, tilting back his head and sniffing.

We are sipping mugs filled with warm condensed milk mixed with powdered carob and honey. The sketchbook with realigned lines is open on the counter we lean against, when I casually tell Jim what he might be smelling.

"You damn thing!" He slams his mug on the counter, rattling the carob jar lid.

"You don't go putting anything around here you wouldn't want to put in yourself," he adds with a fire that won't extinguish my stupidity after I tell him about the d-Con capper.

The chink over my bed holds fast. As did the last rites of rodents squirming in metabolic agony—bleeding internally to death, their tormented carcasses putrefying under the sunbaked roof.

We leave our sticky, dredged cups on the counter beside the carob jar. I carry the cooler inside then open the windows and prop the door agape to air out the cabin. As we walk down the road I can't outdistance the penetrating rotting rodent stench blanketing my nostrils with bad karma.

At the building site we continue to confer over my drawings and expand the penciled scale with lines drawn in the dirt by boot tips and branches. Soon we have sketched out a fourteen-by-fourteen area parallel to the slope and Jim haunches down where I plan to cut a door into wall logs yet to be raised.

As we sit in the imaginary door jamb, Jim pulls a bread chunk from his breast pocket. It is wrapped in a piece of brown grocery sack. He unwraps it, smooths out the paper, and breaks the bread, handing me half. We chew on this stove-top bread, thick as a paperback novel, dense as hardtack. I'd learned to make this whole grain bread while I was building the cabin and it became a staple of my diet. Now, because of the bears these staples—the groats, wheat, and rye berries used in hand-ground flour—are in the toilet. Fortunately, Jim is willing to break his loaf with me.

Though it has been months since we've worked together for any great length of time, our talk retains the flavor of the familiarity of the woods in which we have worked together building the cabin. Without Jim's knowledge, skill and strength I most likely would have either quit or died trying to build my log home. I won't rely on him as heavily to build my bear-proof cellar with a studio on top but I know from experience that what I'm getting into will require his guidance from the ground up.

After lunch we stake out the foundation with yellow string pulled taut around boulders and pine limb spears. Unlike the cabin, the main floor will be supported on a square cement cellar dug five feet into a parfait of alluvium till and sedimentary deposits. Posts will support the porch flooring with a wide open view. Now that my building plans are more resolved than before we ate unleavened bread in a phantom doorway, Jim calls it a day and we walk up to his truck parked above the budding building site.

He backs around on a level spot I cleared with a squared-off shovel and drives away. Walking up to the cabin I mull over the daunting task of digging a hole deep as I am tall, my pondering kicked to the curb by the sight ahead.

Didn't we leave those on the counter? One blue tin mug lies sideways on the step. Another on the porch. Novice gumshoe that I am, the evidence before me prompts a jump into the truck. I roll up the window and blare the horn, hoping this will flush out the tin cup mover, which I assume from recent experience is a bear and more than likely to be inside the cabin.

Within minutes the cab is broiling as I stew about what to do—confront the intruder or drive away to live in a place where wild animals are secured by leads and cages and the only bears are smiley plastic containers filled with honey. The keys are in the ignition but my wallet is inside the cabin. Without a license or money I'd get as far as Emery would extend lunch-counter credit.

Leaning on the horn long enough to worry the battery low I think about locating the nearest weapon. There is a lug nut wrench, jack handle, and a ratty Rand McNally Road Atlas behind the bench seat.

Folded in half, the atlas keeps the hinge and frame ajar in case of a needed retreat. Outside the cab I gather an arsenal of pine cones and rocks, then hurl them onto the porch, hoping to scare out an as-yet unseen intruder.

Nothing stirs. Cautiously I approach the cabin, armed with a tire-jack handle. Peeking around the door, determining the coast is clear I see the floor and sink counter on the other hand are not. The carob jar has been knocked over and emptied, soft brown powder everywhere. The cooler has also been upended and the cabin stinks like dead rats.

Mentally the goal seems attainable, but I discover that chipping out a bear-proof cellar is on par with chinking—mindless drudgery I'd performed on the cabin that involved troweling mortar between logs, one gap at a time. Now digging a cellar, shovel by shovel, is about the same and it is difficult to envision an end after hours of callused Herculean labor results in only an ankle-deep trench.

That first day of digging sets the tone for the weeks to follow. I am on site at nine sharp and pick and shovel until one o'clock when I stop for lunch—an apple and cheese noshed by the branchy, screened creek. After the third day I quit bringing a book to read on break because it is too easy to be hooked by a page-turner and put excavation on the back burner.

I've taken to shouldering the loaded thirty-thirty everywhere except when I'm behind a pick and shovel. The heavy rifle, loaded, safety off, is always within reach. But I've yet to be bothered by bear while I'm nicking my way to China.

A week of digging produces a dirt berm that rims a nearly calf-high pit. This earthy rise makes it impossible to pitch up dirt over the lip and it must be whittled down in the same matter it was laid up, one shovel at a time.

After two weeks the cellar is not quite a foot and a half deep, my bare back is brown as a deer and I'm teetering on the brink of desolation. Hitting a deeply-rooted fir stump, smack in the middle of the pit, reminds me that I resolved to paint and to draw this summer and not to work like a link in a chain gang.

One lunch break I squish Oregon grape berries on my thigh, spreading and etching the pigment with a twig. The message is this: it's time to put down the shovel and pick up a brush.

Besides this 80-acre mountain side, a trashy trailer, ten-speed bike, and used trucks, the other biggest investments I've ever made include an Echo chainsaw and a French easel. The saw with its twenty-inch bar is a perfect fit, so is the easel after a cobbler grommeted leather backpack straps to the frame. Since I returned to the cabin I'd fired up the saw but not the easel.

When I first enrolled in community college, I checked art as a major. Not because I was, nor wanted to be, an artist, but because I always drew and Art was on the top of an alphabetized list of what counted as an undergraduate major.

In the Eugene college one of these matriculated classes, Painting 101, was instructed by a man I'll name Mr. P. to protect his anonymity and the fact he had been moved from the accounting or math department to head the art department when the college experienced a teacher shortage. His unique painting style, he informed the class, encompassed applying layer after layer of (oil or acrylic, I can't remember) glaze to create depth in his paintings. Mr. P. numerated each veiled coat with a penciled check mark on the back side of the canvas he tilted before curious students, so we could see through his layers…of nonsense I believed.

"Sixty-four in this one," he said holding up a painting of a wall clock, the industrial kind commonly found outside of an elementary school principal's office. Simple in composition, that painting, like its stout maker, also lacked any depth, even to the uneducated eye. Still, like babies responding to bright colors and simple shapes, the students praised the accountant's artwork, perhaps hoping to increase the chance of bettering their grade in his class.

The accountant's first assignment was to paint two white Styrofoam blocks, foreground to a flaccid American flag. Diligent beginners planted their easels in a half moon around this set up. I stood back and studied the subject matter staged in a corner of the classroom then flat-out turned to the window and looked out upon the subject that mattered to me, rolling hillsides flush with wildflowers.

Pocketing brushes and tubes of acrylic paint, a stretched canvas under arm, and a bucket of water in hand, I turn my back on this academic façade and walk out of the class, down a corridor, push open two glass doors and head toward a grassy knoll, just beyond the campus. Ladybugs and caterpillars didn't seem bothered as my butt planted upon their foraging ground. I stretched out, set a palette then got to painting lupine and lilied swales. Outside I was in my element. Inside the studio I was marked absent.

At the weekly critique, my landscape was blatantly distinguished amid twenty-three paintings of Styrofoam, red, white and blue. The guy at the easel beside me received an A and an award for his still life. I received an incomplete. It would be the last class I ever took for that kind of credit.

Painting landscapes is what I'd intended to do this summer but fear of bears kept me close to the cabin with a door to shut for safety. This fear shifted a bit one early rainy evening. Because I hadn't seen any bear for a couple of days it seemed safe to paint in the great outdoors where there wasn't a hinge in sight.

Inipi trails me but hesitates before the log bridging a frothing stretch of creek. I unshoulder the rifle, then the easel and carry that cat over rapids sure to drown one of his lives if he twisted free of my arms. Safe on the other side he waits as I return for my gear. We head up a pine-needly incline and I set up the easel under a juniper ten or twenty times or more my senior, select a view and squeeze out a palette.

It feels awkward at first to hold a nimble brush and not a stocky gun butt, pick, or shovel. But after a few strokes I quit thinking about the discrepancy in the tools I'm grasping or how I should begin this painting and just start messing about with color until I quit thinking.

Marbling purple shadows and blood-red highlights mix into tangerine-frosted mountainsides, tripping my sense of realism with exaggerated color intensity. As if ramping up hues on canvas will transfuse similar brilliance in me, I paint until the sun sinks down behind ranges and ranges west of my arid roost and imagine it slipping into an ice-blue Pacific Ocean I cannot see.

In the waning afterglow, I fold up the easel then secure the canvas, the painting resolved enough to stand on its own, but lacking refinement enough to conclude it finished. After it dries, I will glaze in more defining highlights and shadows, a Flemish technique I picked up from studying art history books and far away from an accountant's classroom. With the image affixed in my memory of what I could not stay to see develop, Cadmium Orange smears the rifle butt as I bend to pick up a scaredy cat and carry him over a log bridging twilight-tinged splashing.

I leave the painting, palette and brushes soaking outside. Either linseed oil and turp fumes act as repellents or those bears are natural born critics. All night the porch stays quiet as a gallery after closing.

12. Familiar History

Fifty percent of my family is dead. The other half is alive and, well, most of the time I don't know where they live.

There was a time when my life was as secure and certain as a nuclear middle-class Catholic family could be in a home as proper as the parents who adored and cared for their three children. Then my father died and home security shifted. When my mother went the way of my father, that foundation fell the way of both my parents six feet under, gone forever. In a heartbeat, at age fourteen, I inherited the middle role in a freshly-minted trio of sibling orphans as broken and disenfranchised as me.

I also inherit that small trust intended for my education when I turned eighteen, a fund eroded by managing embezzlers. At seventeen I hired an attorney to protect what was willed to me. Years later I am still fighting and paying to stay in what is a fiduciarily-weighted losing battle.

Instead of spending the funds on a matriculated diploma I bought a deed attached to eighty wild acres. This teenage real-estate transaction also qualified me to advise my teenaged siblings to, "buy land, before you spend all your inheritance on things that will either kill you or get you jailed."

The year after I purchased my land, my brother Mark followed my suggestion and bought forty acres about four or five mountain drainages west of my place, depending on how deep a draw is measured.

A year later my sister Ann responded to a letter I sent her and bought eighty acres half a mile below my property, with that dilapidated cabin I lived in briefly while building my own cabin. Even though she was my closest neighbor, she came and went unpredictably, so I rarely saw her. My brother was another story.

For the first time since "orphaned" stamped our lives and we were all separated, we once again claimed residences in one county. At eighteen, nineteen, and twenty years old, we collectively owned 200 acres as remote as the values and security that had once stabilized our childhoods.

A picture of our past is preserved on the top bookshelf in the cabin, in a framed photograph of the happy unit we once were. We were posing for a stranger solicited to shoot a still with one of my mother's Leica cameras. It's a freeze-frame of our family history in San Francisco, typified by Sunday brunches at the Top of the Mark or Jack Tar after a holy stint in Saint Patrick's. Our church clothes are off-gassing the incense of high-mass and oily perfume-drenched arthritic grandmas too crippled to genuflect before cathedral pews. A mink stole snaps around my mother's pearl-throated neck. My father and brother are dressed sharply in suits and ties. My sister and I sport white patent leather shoes and identical, mother-sewn, frilly dresses.

Today this tableau of my family is as vacuous as the inside of my rural mailbox, as out of touch as a 747 jet in overhead flight.

Now my family connection consists of aging wayfaring orphans who come and go and collide on this mountainside only by infrequent coincidence.

Since returning, I'd neither heard from nor seen my brother or sister. None of us had a phone. We are communicatively untethered, connecting with each other through hand-written letters and notes cached inside a mailbox rusting at the end of a graveled road seven miles below my cabin. Except for the weekly Bi-Mart insert it is usually empty.

Any semblance of a familial connection in my life is growing inside a red-painted log cabin three miles below my cabin. The Nelsons, a big and big-hearted Mormon family cramped that space but they always had room for me. Just knowing them filled a hole hollowed in me the day my last parent was deep-sixed.

One morning, hungry for companionship, I put the aluminum pail on my head, shouldered the rifle and set out to visit the Nelsons. Past the goshawk nest I remove the pail and three miles later, I lean the rifle against the outside wall before knocking on the mudroom door Rhonda opens. We catch up on the local news which is not as substantial as the lunch I help her fix and serve. At noon, like clockwork, Rhonda's husband and kids file in and sit down to eat a meal I am invited to share. Glen bows his fatherly head and begins grace with, "Dear Heavenly Father we are thankful…" and he goes on until an "Amen" concludes the prayer and eating begins.

The Nelson's kitchen is not a fancy restaurant with finger bowls. Everyone here wears traces of ranching and logging on their played-out work clothes, not the shine and elegance of cufflinks and ruffles. Buckets, jugs and containers on the counter are evidence of the milking, butchering and egg collecting that goes on daily. The stove is cool to touch only at night when bedroom lights go out. This kitchen is the heartbeat of a neighborly family developing in my life as blood family fades in a photograph on a shelf.

On the hike home, I juggle a jar of peaches Rhonda has given to me, tossing it high and twirling once before it lands in my open hands. Miles later I set the jar down to put the pail on my head and spy blazing new yellow surveyor tags tied to branch tips distant from the goshawk tree. After positioning the pot so it doesn't obscure my vision, I march on by one hand pumping a Mason jar, the other weaving a rifle back and forth—and imagine the flickering tape is confetti.

I am a majorette, marching to my own tune in this parade of one I am leading on.

13. Bear Trap

From the porch—the stage for a folly never fully played—I watch Don Paulsen ride into the flaming sunrise. When mount and mule are around the bend, I climb the loft ladder and lie down. In the last two nights I can count on one hand the number of hours I've slept. This dawn I'm hoping to add a finger or two.

On Wednesday, after a morning spent splitting wood, hauling water and tidying up the cabin, I dig out the studio site until mid-day. Though bone-tired by then I decide to go to town for supplies and to take the Echo to the repair shop because it has developed a croaking trend. Mostly, I want to check for mail. Even a Bi-Mart sales insert would be a welcome sight in a rusting mailbox hard pressed to present its red, metal flag for anything but junk advertisements.

Before leaving that afternoon, as a precaution against marauding bears, I wedge a two-by-four up against the cabin door and the porch rail. Planning to be back before dark I leave the rifle beside the stove.

Adding to my usual go-to-town itinerary—laundry, library, groceries, gas—I stop by the Department of Fish and Wildlife to ask if they might set up a live trap near my cabin.

"No. It's all in your hands," says the uniformed man behind a government-issued desk.

Until that summer on the mountain I'd only crossed paths with elk and deer, once a pygmy rabbit and it died of fright the second we sighted one another. But never bears. The bruins bothering me that summer were not born on the mountain. These bears, I learned in the office, were likely rogue, dumpster-diving, camp-robbing animals tranquilized in a national park before being relocated to my neck of the woods where they continued their habituated foraging.

Because of that extra stop I don't have time to take the Echo to the doctors and head home weighed down by a loaded pack and the prospect of what is in my hands. Even though I checked the mailbox on the way into town, I check it again. It is still as empty as I am beginning to feel.

By the time I've parked below the cabin it is still light enough to see food strewn over the porch and down the steps and the two-by-four lying beside the open door. I blare the truck horn until sunset then move, armed with a tire jack, from one door jamb through another.

Inipi must have snuck in after the bears jimmied the door and ransacked the cooler. When I discover him curled in the loft bed with a *Don't bother me* kind of half-eyed stare I secretly wish he acted more like a dog than a pampered puss. A dog would never take a catnap amidst this gamey mischief. A dog might have scared off or even chased off the bear that did this.

I place pulverized tomatoes, lettuce and bananas along with the restocked cooler inside the truck bed and turn the camper shell handle tight, figuring the fresh and spoiled food will be safer there. After tidying up I bring the fire poker into the loft and lie rigid beside an oblivious ball of fur.

The next morning I wake to one of those ponderosa pine, fresh-baked-sugar-cookie smelling, bird-chirping mornings that awakens my senses and an appetite. Refreshed by sleep and a hot breakfast I almost levitate down to the pit where the first thing I do is find myself wondering how to remove a stump.

Stretching out the green heavy-duty nylon rope, I'm wondering if it is long enough to loop through a wood pulley then toss it over a nearby pine branch. Dan sold me the antique, still useable after a good oiling and steel-wool rub down.

I'm figuring to lash one rope end around the stump, the other end around my waist, then stand on a boulder above the pit and jump into it. My displaced weight, I'm hoping, will be equivalent to the force required to uproot the root. Before I have the chance to fully test my extraction theory, Don Paulsen appears on the scene putting my guesswork to rest.

Usually he doesn't visit until the evening so I figure he's either bored or in trouble at home. Since I don't have time to stand around slack-jawing, I ask him to help me out. I also ask him if he is missing a horse. No. But he knows the one I'm asking about because he too had to shoo it away from the rose-hip gate to get through. It's a Belgium draft horse and freshly shoed he says. It's an observation I do not question; this man knows his mounts.

Don vetoes my plan by telling me I'd likely be cut in half at the waist or left hanging if I enacted my brand of stump removal. Ditching the stretchy nylon rope, he uses the lariat on his mule's tack, hitches it around the stump, the other around his saddle horn. Spitting sluice along with directions, Don convinces Maggie with kind words and not a whip.

Maggie strains forward then is pulled back by the weight of the stump. While Don coaxes the mule, I alternate spade wedging with a mattock to chop away at taproots. Maggie manages steady straining until the stump gives like a slow and stubbornly-pulled tooth. We cut remaining roots in the pulpy cavity until the stump is fully freed. Don re-lashes the rope to the saddle and Maggie pulls it out of the pit and over the berm lip. I thank Don for his help, aware that it won't be the last I see of him that day.

Dusk brings its familiar ozone scent. It's a rapture of atmosphere, simmering down from sizzling day to shivering night; a sugary, metallic breeze aerated by a frothing creek. I'm leaning over the porch rail inhaling this when I catch a whiff of a mule and a man equipped to kill.

I had told Don about the most recent bear break-in and he has come to make good on a promise to "Get that varmint fer ya." We off-load saddle bags and assemble the contents—a jar of honey, a paper bag filled with oats, an old paint pail, a ball of string, and a cow-bell.

I stand by the creek and watch Don build a little rock pyre, fill the pail with oats, pour honey on top, then balance the luring vessel atop the boulder tripod. He knots string to the pail handle, un-spooling the roll as he walks back to the cabin and looping it over a nail on the porch rail. I remain at the creek, squatting beside this booby-trapped lair and singing a low, remorseful song to the bear we plan to lure.

"Give her a try!" Don yells from the porch.

I jerk the string tied to the pail. The cowbell attached to the other end, clangs. It's a Rube Goldberg device, a leveraged adaptation that—as Don keeps insisting—"Will get that varmint." His theory is that the bear, attracted to the honeyed oats, will nose into the bucket, causing it to tip, jerking the string, ringing the bell and alerting us in plenty of time for us to aim both a flashlight and a rifle.

"Works fine!" Don yells from the porch.

By now it is dark. There is not even a glimmer of new moon to guide my feet along a path patterned by soles picking the softest route. Inside, we

arrange ourselves beside the fire and wait to participate in an event string-
ing our reactions to the creek.

Don settles in the rocker, the rifle primed for action leans next to the
door. I pull up a stump beside him, a flashlight at my feet. We drink black
coffee. Real coffee I boil from Folgers grounds. Coffee, "Thick as mole asses,"
Don declares. By the second cup I have heart palpitations.

We pass time tying knots. Don demonstrates with Manila rope. I practice on a spun nylon piece, a half-hitch, square and some knot that unties
in one pull. Twice a false alarm sends us to the porch, poised for action, but
it's just a breeze that tinkles the bell.

Without invitation, Don tells me stories that never made it into Oregon's
history books as he demonstrates over and over how easy it is to lash a square
knot. There's a story about diggin' a well, and the night wolves attacked his
donkey—an animal, he declared, that was "more ornery than any three
mules put together."

Then he launched into the outhouse tale.

"When I was only three, I fell through the hole. Never, ever will forget
that smell." He scrunches his nose and loops one rope end to another.
"There. See how easy." He sets his knot next to his cup on the corner of
my stump.

I put another log on the fire and wonder how a toddler gets out of deep
shit, but won't ask as it will only prolong the story.

"Roped me out," Don offers with no encouragement on my part. "Mah'
uncle dropped his lasso down and pulled me up." He rocks back and forth
and continues.

"My auntie, by the name of Thelma—I called her Auntie Hellma, cause
she'd switch me for no good reason." Don pauses, thrusts his thumbs inside
the waist of his jeans and leans into the firelight. "Well, she wasn't so lucky."

"You mean your aunt fell into an outhouse too?" I close the fire screen,
wishing I could go upstairs to sleep but knowing I have to stay awake.

"No. When she went to do her business, a black widow bit her where
the sun don't shine. Her hinny swelled so big," Don slurps his coffee, "she
couldn't sit down for a week."

I'm worn down by tying knots and listening to Don unravel stories as
questionable as the authenticity of the cougar penis bone always in his hip
pocket. To keep awake I mix up some corn bread, bake it in the Dutch oven
covered in stove coals. We eat it hot, covered with runny honey drizzled out
of the jar nearly emptied over oats.

Twice we go out to the porch just to check on the bell which remains ready for action that doesn't come that night. By dawn, the coffee pot is as drained as me and the bread is gone. As I'm also hoping Don will soon be.

Maggie spent the night hitched to rock jack below the cabin to hide her scent. Don pats her dewy hide and straps on a saddle and semi-empty saddle bag. After they leave I lie down in the loft, shaking from lack of sleep and too much caffeine. I wake just as jittery two hours later, after seven o'clock.

There's only time for a face splash in the creek because I have to meet Jim's friend down by the green metal gate in half an hour. Jake Richards agreed to loan me lumber for forms, but doesn't know his way up here. He is sitting in his truck when I arrive on foot just before eight.

After a "Good morning," and a friendly handshake I get in the passenger side and we drive on. At the rose-hip gate the mystery horse greets us then bolts after I soundly repeat, "Yah! Git! Yah! Git!"

That horse found a shortcut I had yet to find and beat us to the building site. He stood in the cellar hollow nuzzling the pulpy, tobacco-seasoned earth around a recently uprooted stump. Jake and I step out of the cab and toss pine cones at his flank until he plods into the woods. We unload the form boards, shouldering then stacking them down the incline. Finished, we walk up to the cabin so I can give Jake gas money. The horse is there rubbing his rump on the east wall, tail swinging like a pendulum before relieving himself just below the steps.

In the afternoon I spread a manure mash around the cabin, reasoning that urine is a known natural repellent so solid waste must be too because both are excreted from neighboring points. The next few hot days dry out the horse apples and I rake sedgy loam around the cabin's perimeter. For the rest of the week there's no hide nor hair of a bear, grizzled or black. Finally, I can sleep again through undisturbed nights and before drifting off I think, *If only life worked as well as horse shit.*

14. Rub a Dub Dub

Besides Anabell and Rhonda I don't have any other women friends in these parts, so it is always nice to chat with Janette in John Day as she dispatches dump trucks. At least twenty years older than me, big-boned and flashing a smile only the lucky are invited to share, she walkie-talkies men hard as what they haul.

Like Emery, this stranger encountered through simple commerce serendipitously befriended me. And like Emery, I looked forward to exchanges with Janette, however brief, because it gave me someone to talk to and alleviated my mostly-unrequited need for feminine communication even if it took place in a rock quarry.

I buy sand and gravel at the pit that Janette manages from the inside of a corrugated metal booth anchored before a chain-link gate she opens every morning at eight and locks precisely at four. Today, while ordering three-quarter ag I hope to unload a heavy heart.

Since returning to the cabin I've been lonely to the bone, scared to the core by bear and have not shared these things with anyone.

After handing her a ten-spot for my order and palming the change, Janette prolongs our monetary transaction by asking, "What cha been up to?"

I lean out of the cab to get a closer look into her workstation. Three Harlequin paperbacks rest beside a walkie talkie, receipt books and a hand-tooled leather purse. One cover is illustrated with a bare-chested man sucking the neck of a woman, her mouth agape like she has swallowed a bee mistaking her uvula for a hive. I must have been staring too long because Janette says, "Hon, you want to borrow that copy?" Before I can answer she hands me the book.

When I drive into the pit to take on another load, I feel lighter because I told Janette about the bear and she listened without offering advice on how to kill it. I am also in possession of a slip of paper with the phone number of a man written on it and a bodice-burning paperback.

Back at the building site, I park Tank as close to the cellar site as is safe and shovel out the bed onto level ground beside the pit. I don't know how soon I'll get around to mixing the ag into cement to pour into forms not yet built to support walls as far from materializing. With the bed swept clean I dig until five and decide to call it a day and get ready to bathe. Stripping down by the creek I hear a motor.

Lately Don has been showing up to visit around the same time nearly every evening and I wish I'd never told him I take a bath every night between five and six. The original hint was meant to let him know I was occupied and didn't want a visitor coming up with excuses of pie or peaches, goat milk, hand-me-down clothes from Orinda or whatever else he might bring along with an ulterior motive.

As the engine grows louder I realize it is not the familiar grumbling emitted from any of the vehicles Don drives. This pitch is smooth, muffled fury and spewing from a monster truck, twice as tall as me, with four sets of searchlights on top. By the time I'm buttoned and zipped two men dressed in woodland camo have gotten out of the truck.

I figure one must be the contact Janette gave me, who I'd called from the pay phone outside of Chester's. Neither one is.

After a brief exchange and, "No, thanks, I don't need your help," the strangers drive away.

Word travels fast in a small town when sentences include bears.

Ten minutes after they are gone I walk down the road and pick up a crumpled cigarette pack and something I've never seen before—a tube about the size and shape tennis balls are sold in, but it bears the label, Pringles, not Wilson.

Like clockwork Don comes chugging up on his tractor, shortly after five. He had showed up earlier in the week to level a road to the building site—an offer I accepted even though I rebuked him for attempting a goodbye kiss. Now he was back with a bathtub and four cinder blocks.

Just what does he take me for anyway…Secondhand Rose?
Whatever.

At this point I'm mystified by Don's newest offering until he explains.

"Ya' dig a pit and set the tub on these here," he says, unloading the cinder blocks by the creek. "Then fill it and build a fire under it."

I did fine bathing in the creek, sudsing up on the bank and rinsing off with an aluminum saucepan, but was willing to give this idea a try.

After he leaves I dig a four-foot-long rectangle, strategically set the cinder blocks, then lift and lower the tub on them. Over the next week, by trial and error, I perfect the art of making and taking a hot bath in the wild.

I sit in the tub, perched on a board weighted down by boulders, buffering my fanny from the searing cast iron bottom (this was the first trial by error). When it gets too hot and before I become a juicy bit in a cannibal stew, I dip out a saucepan of cold water from a nearby bucket. A bottle of Johnson's Baby Shampoo, a bar of Castile Soap and the rifle within arm's reach complete the toiletry.

Bathing after dusk one evening a hair-raising shriek gets me seizing the gun and running naked, trailing suds back to the cabin. Toweling off on the safety of the porch I strain to see the cougar that never shows itself across the creek.

15. Karma

If only this old rocker could console me like my mother once did. "There, there, everything will be all right," she would say, calming me in her lap, nursing bruises and skinned knees and the full spectrum of childhood accidents and fevered diseases.

Like my nurturing mother, the bothersome bear is gone.

All alone, curled into this rocking family heirloom, I nurse a sickening grief set in my chest like concrete.

There is no cure for this dis-ease.

I have only myself to hold.

Accountable.

My heart is sick because I shot a bear, a bloody bone fragment in my breast pocket to prove it.

Only that morning I was contently rocking away, reading and waiting for it to get light enough to go outside. When the eastern sky blazes dawning, I close my book, shoulder the rifle, venture outside and confront more than the call of nature.

How'd that there? I wonder until what looked like a stump, swivels and mews adorable as all get out.

A black cub, nonplussed, bats me a Bambi-eyed look that makes me wonder why this character is not on the set of a Disney movie instead of the outhouse path. If it could talk, I knew that baby bear would be saying, "Rub my belly." I remain slack-jawed as low morning light casts a halo around a pelt that warrants a rollicking cuddle and not a steely muzzle.

The rifle presses into my shoulder blade as I figure this cub, anthropomorphic, cute as a bug, must have a musky mother in the vicinity. An assumption borne out when I get a whiff of something that turns me as fast in my tracks as a big black bear lumbers downhill, straight toward the cub and me. There is no time to unstrap or level the rifle barrel. I break into a run, bolting toward the cabin, slamming the door, then leaning against it, shaking with nerves ragged as my breath.

Still panting, I drag the ladder up into the loft then steady myself against the dormer. I point the rifle barrel out the open window and fire. The warning shot rings in my ears long after scaring Inipi into hiding.

For over an hour I stay in the loft, thumbing through old magazines and thinking that tin trailer in Eugene seems like paradise past. I decide at any time in my life I'd rather confront a constipated toilet and care for hungry hobos over facing a mama bear at my log cabin.

By mid-morning I cannot put off business any longer, move to the porch, aim and fire toward the outhouse. When nothing comes charging out of the piney yonder I set about my routine.

Primed with fear, I split wood, slop water buckets from the creek, and jump at the slightest snap of a branch or stretch of forest shadow. Even Inipi is uptight and still won't get near me when I am strapped to the rifle.

In the afternoon I go to fill two kerosene lamps in the fuel shed and cross paths with the cub again. It is as adorable as when I'd seen it earlier that morning and we stare at each other until a low, hollow, cat-like moo breaks our bonding and a bigger bear bounds from behind the shed.

I sail over dropped kerosene lamps, yank open the wonky door and dive into that bat-and-board, five-foot-square shed.

For nearly an hour I pass the time reading. Shelved literary distractions include smeared Penzoil 30-30 and Echo Bar and Chain Oil labels on cardboard cans and plastic bottles. By the time I've read the fine print three or four times over, the smell of petroleum products is as irritating as the sweltering heat stirring sweat from my skin and snapping tamarack shakes overhead. I open the door for a breath of fresh air and to check if the coast is clear.

This is the moment I decide it is either me or the bear and that I have to kill one if I do not want to end up like that lady in Alaska.

After I fill the dropped lamps—amazingly they are not broken—I make a special trip to town hoping to persuade the Department of Fish and Game man.

He refuses again, to send up dogs or to set up a live trap. The only thing he gives me is counsel. If bears are bothering me on land I own then I have the right to kill them. I don't mention that I am a borderline vegetarian and that sacrificing an animal is not on my property-rights menu.

Back at the cabin, I nail two-by-fours just below shoulder height on both ends of the porch to steady the barrel and practice sighting, primed to shoot whatever moves even if it is a fir needle wafting. When it gets too dark to see I go inside and light two brimming lamps.

In the morning I assume my porch perch, a cup of whatever matching the time of day in one hand, a book in the other. Safety off, the rifle on my lap, prepared to shoot even the breeze.

I have a habit. Each month I select one area or one author and read as much as possible written about a subject or by a writer. I do this for thirty days exactly. I began this practice when I was old enough to have a library card and check out chunky chapter books.

By age seven I burned through Keene, Hope and Appleton. I spent the entire sixth grade Christmas vacation tackling Robert Louis Stevenson, reading every page of *Treasure Island*, and *The Strange Case of Dr. Jekyll and Mr. Hyde*, only skimming *The Master of Ballantrae*, and nearly finishing *New Arabian Nights* when the Times Square ball dropped into a new year. At age seventeen I read every book I could find on gangsters.

This June is my May Sarton month. I've thumbed the life out of *Journal of Solitude* trying to justify my own. *The Fur Person* and *The Poet and the Donkey* were fast romps compared to *Mrs. Stevens Hears the Mermaid Singing*, which I'm paging through. I've given up on seeing a bear when one ambles across the creek in dead range of my literary post. Unlike the baby or the mama this one has a gray muzzle and it pauses mid-stream.

I stand, legs spread wide, barrel steady, and slowly squeeze the trigger but release it without firing after the bear sniffs and retreats into snowberry and willow cover. If I'd shot the instant it turned tail, most likely it would have only been hit in the butt.

It is nearing late afternoon when the west end of the porch hits full sun and I strip down to cutoffs. Mrs. Stevens is beginning to bore me so I resume *Journal of Solitude*.

"You don't really escape feeling. You just get a big slap in the face from it."

Oh, those self-absorbed writers, writing about feelings. They're writing because they've got time to self-reflect, I think, an open book and rifle pressuring my bare thighs. *There are more relevant things to address in life than to write about or to ponder soulful reasoning. Feed starving children. Stop baby seal slaughter. Straighten out crooked politicians. Castrate convicted rapists.*

Incarcerate corrupt politicians. Pay public school teachers the equivalent of NFL, NBA, MLB players.

Before my convoluted contemplations advance or the weight of the rifle cuts off circulation to my calves, I see another bear across the creek. It is not Gray-muzzle. This bear is smaller, blacker. Like its predecessor it stops mid-creek, snout proud. Softly I put down the book down, inch to a stand, and level the barrel. Elbows to my side, holding my breath, like I do when composing final touches on an oil painting with a triple 000 sable brush, I apply the trigger.

The bear rears up upon impact of the shell rocketing a distance too rapid to clock on my shelved Timex. Our eyes lock in surprise before the animal crumples on all fours, falters upright, shakes its head, and gives me a stare like "I didn't warrant a steely muzzle." Like its predecessor it disappears through low bank brush. I don't know if that black bear is male or female. But I'm sure it isn't dead.

Rifle in hand, I sail down the porch steps and am halfway to the creek when I remember reading that an injured bear will feign death then attack if provoked. I'd certainly just initiated the first act and am primed to enact its demise. But rationality prevails and I turn back to the cabin, button into a shirt and lace on tennis shoes. Tank has been sitting under the sun all day and doesn't need warming up when I drive it down the mountain, leaving the gates wide open.

Orinda opens the door. Before she invites me in, I've crossed the threshold and am dialing the wall mounted rotary. "I shot a bear!" I yell across the living room then repeat into the receiver, "I shot a bear." I register a "Hullo," before I add, "and it's not dead! Can you come up and help me get it?"

It is my problem and fine for me to finish what I've started because the Fish and Game man won't leave his office, is the official reply. Looking down upon my dusty tennis shoes, adrenalin is losing its punch as the question of what to do next takes precedence over my predicament.

"Why don't you just stay the night?" Orinda's face softens with concern as I cradle the avocado-green handset attached to a curly cord nearly stretched straight.

Don rises from the dining room chair where he was listening to my telephone conversation. Without a word he dials the phone still warm from my concerned call. Seconds later he gets to talking. "Need help getting that varmint." A few minutes later we are walking out of the pantry, Don armed with a rifle, to meet Glen Nelson at the fork in the road.

Glen and two of his sons and their dog follow behind in another truck as I drive to the cabin. Don, beside me, pats my knee. "Don't worry, Sweetheart. We'll get that varmint." I shift down to second and push his hand away.

I'm as tired out by Don's wandering mitts as I am by his reference to bears as varmints. A varmint, to me, is a gnawing rat or a conniving crook. This bear I shot is neither. It is habituated wildlife I've provoked with a bullet.

We walk to the spot where the bear dropped on all fours. The men stand in shallow riffles, water cascading over their work boots. I perch on a boulder because I can't see the point in getting my tennis shoes wet.

Glen bends over and picks something off a blood-stained boulder, holds it at arm's length. "Looks like a rib bone." He drops the fragment then focuses on the other side of the bank, walks across the creek then stoops to pick up a stick. Like the grass where it laid, it is covered in blood. He holds it in front of the dog who sniffs it like he has chased cattle five years too long.

I pick up the smudged bone Glen tossed, pocket it, then leapfrog across slick rocks to join the men. We pair off. The Nelson boys go upstream. I stay with Glen, Don and the dog.

As we bushwhack, Glen explains that a wounded animal will stay near water. Don concurs as both have hunted for years and have on occasion only nicked their target. We take the north and the boys hike up the south side of the creek. The dog trails me as I follow the men.

For nearly two hours we hardscrabble among rocky caverns and cliffs. Glen tosses the bloody stick when the bone-tired dog is clipped to a lead and pulled along instead of leading us. I have to pee but am as hesitant to ask the men to stop and wait as I am to find karma lurking behind a privacy bush.

Nearing dusk, Glen points his rifle up and pulls off three shots, signaling his boys to come back. Within the tail end of that evening hour we all meet up again at the creek where we began this fruitless chase. We regroup on the bottom porch steps, sharing our profitless tracking stories, eagerly drinking tin mugs of creek water freshly drawn and sloshing in a bucket beneath our stoop. The dog is spread-eagled in the dirt, pooped.

Don declares to our little group, "This woman sure knows how to use a gun." An affirmation and a counterfeit badge of courage I do not want to be pinned to.

"Lavon," Glen puts his hand on my shoulder, "Ya come on down and stay a night or two. That bear won't get far. Most likely it will bleed out before it dies of infection in this heat."

I politely refuse the invitation and mull on his sagely advice. Being in proximity of mortally wounded wildlife seemed more my comeuppance.

In bed that night, I lie awake not knowing if the bear is mortally wounded and cowering in bloody shock in some rocky outcrop, or rigor mortis stiff under the stars.

On the foam mattress in my log cabin loft, my body clenched hard as a fist, I tried to palm an elusive sleep. Squeezing my eyelids tight I couldn't shut out the sight of the bear or the empathetic part of me also mortally wounded that day. The part of me who will in a flash dash across traffic lanes to rescue strayed or injured cats and dogs. Once a chipmunk, like the others, tire marked and lingering on its way to roadkill as I cradled its calamity. The dogs and cats whimpered and whined, the chipmunk though went without a peep. "There, there, little baby. Little baby, there, there," I'd repeat as each animal labored its last bubbly, bloody, breath in my lap.

Now, I had deliberately crossed the line.

The next morning morbidity hangs in the air, so thick even the juncos can't cut a tweet, the chipmunks a cheep. The forest is shaming me. Sorrow seeps between every evergreen needle, it flows down the creek and eddies in my chest. All I can do is sit on the porch and stare at the spot where I shot the bear. An American Dipper lights on the rock that briefly balanced a bloody rib bone then flies away as if spooked.

The next day I am still too distraught to move much or to concentrate on a page.

May Sarton never wrote about feeling like this. I decide a trip to town is better than wallowing in remorse. When I return that evening I place fresh groceries in a burlap sack slung over a cottonwood by the creek. In the morning the sack is down. Overnight my food supply is reduced to a jar of instant coffee and a few cans of tuna and green beans.

On the third night after the shooting, I go to bed with an emptiness I try to satisfy by reading a borrowed Harlequin. Until then I'd only eyeballed the covers of a genre of books I never once had the desire to crack open. Tonight is different. Heartache prompts me to find consolation behind a lusty book cover. But by chapter two, as much as I might subliminally want to mimic the heroine's fiery erotic urgency tendered in gently plucked nipples, I bookmark literal foreplay knowing I need my shut-eye if I am going to handle a man in the morning.

Bruce is not alone. Though I'd spoken to him on the phone outside of Chester's he gave no specific time or date on which he would arrive. I was drinking my first cup of coffee when I heard a truck outside. I took a hasty look in the mirror to see if I was presentable before opening the door and stepping into the wee morning light. After he identified himself, he introduced me to his friend, Charlie, who limps because of a logging accident. "The best part of getting busted up," he says with a grin, "was I married my nurse."

The men drink mugs of water I've extended as they outline how they will work the dogs. In the time it takes to drain their cups I've learned that the dogs yapping and rocking inside plywood kennels have been trained to follow their noses, their long snouts and droopy ears aid in keeping animal scents close to their face. I like dogs better than cats, but I don't take to these dogs because they have been trained to dish out what they've taken.

One by one Bruce unlatches each caged dog and in a flash four rawboned bloodhounds dash about and bay up a canine storm parallel to none until Bruce kicks one in the butt. Dogs normally don't scream, but the kicked one does and the other three dogs downsize their yowling.

"Guess I kicked him a little too hard."

Fresh blood rims the anus of one quieted-down dog.

"Got anything with a scent?" Bruce asks after scuffing his boot in the dust.

I climb onto the porch and drag the Coleman down the steps, then shove the cooler toward Bruce and notice his boot tip is tainted with what he dissed.

Bruce lets the pack draw scent from the ice chest. Through voice commands he leads the dogs to the creek where they match the scent from the Coleman with the smell of old and new paw prints. Bruce says you can tell how fast a bear is traveling by the toes, whether they point up or down, and how fresh the track is by the dew in the print. Whether there was dew in these new impressions or they were just moist from the creek bank, I didn't know, but the toes were pointing up hill.

With a single "Get em!" four howling hounds follow Bruce's direction, sail through the creek and scale the serpentine, pine-needle incline. Charlie is the first to follow, Bruce trailing him, me last in line.

By the time the men catch up with the dogs and I catch up with the men we are all panting above a deer kill raft of brown hair tufts, putrefying viscera, a disjointed leg and spine. The skull is only partially shredded, eyes eaten away. Charlie looks around and toes into a dark pile outside the kill's immediate periphery.

"Bear scat," he explains. The deer could have been downed by a coyote, but most likely a larger predator like a cougar. When they had their fill, bears moved in, dragging carrion to the creek because they liked to wash their food. When they were finished with the deer, they had moved on to my sunken refrigerator and porched cooler. Once the food chain is gone, Charlie says, the bears move on. He picks up a leg, bits of fur and flesh clinging to the bone, waves it in front of the dog's noses. "Get em."

Even with all the pins, plates and screws securing his left ankle, fibula and tibia, Charlie charges up the steep draw, Bruce at his heels. Even though I am a runner, I can't keep pace and they, rightfully, will not slow down for me. When I'm out of breath and dogs and men are out of sight, I give up the chase and return to the cabin porch to paint, from memory, a portrait of a bear.

By the time Charlie and Bruce reappear with the dogs in a tangle of tugging leashes, I've finished the oil sketch, except for the highlight in the pupils. Plunking the finishing brush in a tin of turp I join them by the truck. Bruce says they found the bear I shot. Freshly dead. He asks if I want to skin it. I don't even own a skinning knife, much less want a fillet of fate. Neither did Bruce or Charlie, their interest solely in running scent hounds.

"You guys want a drink?" I pull two beers out of the cooler, hand them over along with a "Thank you."

"No need for thanks," says Charlie, guzzling and urping after a long pull.

Then he says flatly the carcass will likely be finished off by cougar in a day or so. I'm staring down at my feet, imagining bear parts mixed with rocks and earth, when Bruce sets the empty bottle on the step and turns to unleash and load the dogs.

"Don't you want to give them a drink?" I hold out the bucket, point to dogs still wound up, foam and spittle rimming their jowls.

"Not until I get them home. It'll just make em' have ta pee."

After they leave I go to the creek, take off my shirt and squat on the bank. While shadows grow long my vocal cords sear, howling out a hollowing sadness. Hot bursts, jerky spurts and gut-wrenching wails pour from my mouth and when I come up for air I hear a vehicle drawing near.

Maybe Charlie and Bruce have changed their minds and they are returning to skin the bear. But the familiar mechanical chugging I'm detecting means I won't be talking to bear trackers but to Don. Shit. I need him like I need another hole in my heart. I splash creek water on my blotchy face and finger comb my hair. Don is standing next to his tractor by the time I arrive at the cabin.

"Evenin' Sweetheart." He holds out a paper sack, gives it to me instead of a hug which I appreciate. "Boys stopped by on their way down. Told me they found the bear."

I open the sack, can't make out what's inside but it looks like a dead rat. Timidly, I reach in but do not touch the bear paw inside.

After Don learned from "the boys" that the bear was dead above the cave, he rode his mule up the abandoned logging road to skin and butcher it.

"Found an arrow in his butt." Don rubs his back side, holds out his hand. "Had grizzle big as my fist all around it."

Great. I shot a wounded animal and added to its man-made misery. I clutch the bag and lean against the porch steps.

"Figure it was about three years old. Maybe weighed a hundred and thirty pounds, not much more." Don loops a finger in his belt and takes a step closer. "Packed out what meat I could. Left the hide after I skinned out a coffee-can worth of grease."

I really don't want to ask Don about bear grease, because it would prolong his visit. But I do because a month earlier I bought a blue and white tin of it to seal my boots and wonder if it's the same stuff.

"Use it to keep rats from chewin' on my tack," Don answers and eyeballs my ax buried in a chopping block by the woodshed, the handle dry and splintered by weather and wear. "Even wipe it on my tools. Rats are afraid of the smell, won't nibble on anything touched by it. Next time you're down I'll give ya' some."

I don't bring up the tin I bought but I wonder if either brand of bear grease also works on old men.

When Don is out of sight long enough I can't hear the tractor I take the paper bag to the creek bank where the bear was shot, gingerly reach in, pull out the paw and hold it like a dead rat, at arm's length.

The black pad is worn shiny as my moccasin soles. Ebony claws wedge into furry phalanges, and dried blood rings the ankle where Don sawed off the foot. It off-gasses a gamey smell I encountered once before, standing next to an old miner in the canned bean aisle of the local grocery store.

I flip the paw over and it fits into my palm, as if we are holding hands backwards. Put it back inside the bag and reluctantly retrieve it again. I hold it out like a live grenade. Or like a little logger Cleopatra, asp in hand. I take in a deep breath then pull it quickly to my chest until one claw pokes the skin above my left breast, punctures deep enough to make me grimace and swallow hard. Swallow the fear that has taken me down.

In the morning I set the bear paw on a shelf below the cabin hoping it will emit the fabled pack-rat-scaring vibes. Dew is drying fast by the time I leave the cabin to try and find what's left of the bear Don butchered. Before making the climb I kneel by a mossy spot near the creek and drink. Bending down for a second lap I spy something that straightens my spine.

I've never seen anything like this before and on closer examination never want to again, that grayish blob flapping over a log upstream. Standing and using a long nearby branch I poke it, jumping back just in case it is alive and can poke back. The blob remains stable except for a hunk waving in the water like a half-beached jelly fish.

Considering the forested environment and recalling my high school biology class, I conclude this is not gelatinous marine life but mammal intestines. Pairing two branches like chopsticks I play out the rotting mass, finagling it to the bank and kick dirt over what did not float downstream. Turning to walk away I glimpse a meaty metatarsal hanging like a wishbone high in a pine tree. More blood-pinked bones scatter upslope and I trail the skeletal remains.

Poor deer. Those hooves no longer meant for walking are still attached to legs that have been broken off ball-and-sockets. This is the kill discovered days before, but missing the gut pile upstream from where I'd recently been drinking. It had been dragged around long enough to become part of the predatory chain, chewed and picked apart by winged and clawed scavengers. Unlike other gnawed and dismembered joints, the spine is fully intact, strung together by sinew drying taut.

Mesmerized by this grizzly alignment it is a while before I register shadows cast by vultures drafting thermos overhead. Had I scared them off or were they circling, anticipating a fresher kill—me or karma uphill?

Before I turned back I made a decision. It was time to buy a gun.

A gun that wouldn't break in two.

A gun powerful enough to own.

Whatever messed with me from now on was going to be looking at the pointy end of a barrel. Given my most recent history with a gun, things could get down right messy.

I drive to Prairie City. On the passenger seat The Blue Mountain Eagle is opened to the classified section.

Wicks Guns: New Used Bought Sold. Faded hand-lettering on a plywood board matches the newspaper's crisply-printed advertisement. The sign is nailed into a bat-and-board building banking what looks like a dried up-creek bed overrun with knapweed and Canadian Thistle. I enter the store that really is an old garage with guns now hanging from hooks that once held rakes, shovels and pruners.

"I want to buy a gun that can kill a bear at three hundred feet," I say to a walrus-looking man hulking beneath a rack of gleaming rifles.

"If you can hit a bear from that far then I'll sell you a gun that can."

I told him I already had, but with a thirty-thirty and it only mortally wounded the animal. He said that was good enough for him, didn't ask me to prove it.

But I could have if he asked, with the piece of rib bone in my pocket.

The man sold me a 200 Savage with a high-powered scope, once owned by a sheriff. I back this up with a .22 long-barrel, six-cylinder Colt coddled in a hand-tooled leather holster, pretty as Janette's purse. I walk out with the rifle and return later, when the background check clears, to pick up the pistol.

I named the Savage Yogi. The Colt, Boo-Boo.

16. Wrapping it Up

"I understand why you wouldn't want some." Orinda pushes a brown wrapped parcel, marked Bear, to the side. "Bear meat tastes like what it ate. And the one you shot been eatin' on a dead deer."

Coming back from town I'd stopped at the Paulsen's to see if they would give me a piece of meat. I could have bought a steak or chop at Chesters, but I required something wild and I knew their freezer was chock-full of it.

Orinda rummages around in this frozen-meat menagerie. Elk, Deer, and Bear are hand printed on wrapped packages precisely organized by color—white, Manila and butcher-paper brown. Packages stacked end to end like decimal-coded shelved books; the call of the wild registered in permanent marker. She nabs a white parcel and hands it over. "Don shot it last fall on the other side of Strawberry. Had to quarter it and pack it out." A whoosh of frosty air rises between us as Orinda slams the freezer lid shut.

That evening I build a fire in the rock ring by the creek, then roast that elk steak on a green willow stick. Except for Anabell's stew and my brother's turkey, this is the first meat I've eaten in years and it all comes back to me.

I was raised a carnivore.

Before my mother died, family meals were built around great slabs—sides, rumps, patties and links of meat. Beef was always served rare—bloody rare, the bloodier the better, as long as it didn't moo. Pork though, always had to be cooked until it wasn't pink. Chicken didn't really count as meat because it wasn't red. Fish paled even more than chicken and was eaten only on Fridays, which added to my religious indigestion.

After my mother died, so did those proper sit-down meals. Still I continued to eat meat without care. Until one day on a visit to a farm I picked up a pink wiggling piglet and, in that instant, gave up pork. When the old farmer giving me a tour stuck my index finger into a newborn calf's mouth, its velvet suckle convinced me to give up beef. When the farmer wedged a bummer inside my jacket, the warming task I'd been assigned persuaded me to give up eating lamb.

That's why I chose elk, an animal I had until this very moment—squatting beside the creek—no prior relationship with. I'd seen their droppings on hoofed trails and on petrified ridges but this was the closest I'd ever gotten to an elk, that chunk of it on the end of a charring stick.

Seared over flamey slivers and bickering embers, the venison wisped charbroil aroma reminiscent of grilled hamburger. I bit into it after it cooled, surprised this meat did not taste gamey but flavored of its sedgey free-ranging territory. It was quite tender and tasty and bite by bite, I ate all of it as I adjusted to an adrenalin surge that wasn't mine, but the elk's fear distilled into flesh, encoded the instant before it fell to the shock of a shell—maybe more than one…I didn't recall Don being a crack shot.

The terror pooled in that elk meat was a visceral prompt reminding me that I feel what I eat. Drink too. Especially alcohol. It's like sodium pentothal—a truth serum. One drink too many and I'll tell you what I think and if it's you should go to hell, I will tell you so and your mother too if she's standing nearby and deserving.

The venison had a similar cathartic effect, except it was telling me off; reminding me that I empathize with animals too much to chew them out.

17. Buster

"Son of a bitch! You mother fucker! Get!" My cheeks bellow profanity strong enough to shock the socks off your mother and her entire family if they were standing nearby and were wearing them. But it's just me and the dumb-ass below the dormer window.

I am mindlessly changing clothes in the loft when the cabin starts to reverberate. A troupe of gang banging bears, perhaps? Nope. Only a mammoth horse, methodically rump-massaging the wall beside the porch steps.

Freshly dressed in a finger-creased flannel shirt and jeans, I descend the ladder then stand, hands on hips, looking down upon that horse, and swear at it more. When that fails to register even a flicker of retreat I wail stove wood; pinging kindling doesn't even rattle that muscled hide. When I throw the empty firewood box at the horse's flank he cranes his humongous head to acknowledge this intervention, then resumes bumping the cabin until I fear it will collapse.

I am still cursing, having exhausted my stove wood supply and figuring what to launch next, when a man runs into view, rope in hand. He huffs up the road claiming the distance between us until I can clearly register that this man who is yelling, "Buster! You fucker!" is my brother.

I'd no idea Mark was on the mountain or that he knew that horse by name. It had been many months since I'd last seen or heard from my wanderlust sibling.

He whirls a rope stiff as wire cable and with a wobbly flick of the wrist releases a lasso that lands beyond the ragged ring of stove wood encircling the horse. Not even acknowledging his sister a good morning, my brother re-coils the rope and half lassos the horse's head bent nibbling sweet grass. It rears up, taking out slack and the rope in Mark's hand.

I draw my flannel shirt tight as if it were a mink stole and I am watching a comedy of errors from the choicest box in the house.

"Buster! You fucker!" he yells again. I am by now assuming that Buster is the horse's name, rather than merely an expletive, as the beast trails a lariat down the road.

My brother brushes his palms together and watches the horse trot away. I invite him in for a cup of coffee and a catch up.

I notice Mark's hair line continues to recede. He seems to be trying to tame his handle-bar mustache and beard across his tanned face.

Over the last year, he tells me, he's been enrolled in a blacksmithing school in Olympia, Washington. Apparently, it issues neither grades nor certificates, just skills uniting fire and metal—infernal artistries aligned with my brother's mercurial make up. He's become a ferrier of sorts and has purchased a gooseneck horse trailer and an animal appropriate to his new rig and trade.

Until today I didn't know horseshoers were called ferriers, and have never heard of a gooseneck trailer. I imagine a downy feathered nape attached to a ball and hitch.

Mark leans against the counter as I pull out a boiling water pot from the stove fire. "He's a Belgian Draft horse. Named him Buster. Bought him in Ontario."

"When were you in Canada?" I pour water into a tin mug then stir in three spoons of Taster's Choice.

"Ontario, Oregon," he corrects.

"Oh. More?"

Mark nods his head and I stir in two extra servings and hand him a cup of coffee stout enough to forge ulcers.

By his third cup of Taster's Choice I learn Mark's gooseneck can house and haul a horse, a man and a passel of blacksmithing and welding tools. The rear compartment is geared for beast and tack but this is where my brother sleeps when he is out shoeing because he leaves Buster to graze freely on the mountainside.

"He's not gelded," Mark says out of the blue.

"I didn't see any gold on him," I reply surprised that my brother would fork out even a red cent to ornate a horse.

"Gelded! Not gilded!" Mark lowers the steaming tin mug, his pearly-white orthodontia-corrected teeth counterpoint to the shag framing his lips.

"It means he gets to hang onto his balls so I can breed him."

That explains the steed's three-foot-long penis and a piss stream strong enough to excite a hydraulic miner.

By the fourth cup of coffee I've learned all about my brother's horse and he's learned about my bear.

I show him the paw.

"What did you use?"

"A thirty-thirty."

"You can't kill a bear with a thirty-thirty." The twang of my brother's tongue sharpens when it gets to talking about triggered weapons. In addition to forging tools he has acquired an arsenal of pistols and rifles. He wraps himself in a range of defensive objects like a security blanket quilted from bullets and barrels. Maybe he hopes weapons will console the boy inside who is still grieving for the father he lost at an age when a cap pistol was all he needed.

I re-tell the shooting the bear story as he fingers the bear paw.

"Can I have it?"

"What are you going to do with it?" I point to the severed foot in my brother's leathery hand.

"Rub it on my tack. The smell keeps critters from chewing on saddles."

I see more of the horse than my brother that summer. While Mark is working up a ferrier circuit, traveling from ranch to ranch and bunking in a goose neck, Buster stays behind, un-gelded, free to run the same mountainsides and meadows where I can no longer run freely.

I was born with tear-drop-sized lungs. A childhood steeped in bronchial ailments—gasping, wheezing or croupy coughing—meant I was not born to run. I finished last in every timed schoolyard PE race, crossing the line as though I had cinder blocks strapped to my breast.

On the mountain I was teaching myself to outrun this asthmatic asylum. The arid wilderness was a natural course to stride out without the punishment of a stopwatch to clock me as a loser.

On the mountain I run in Minnetonka moccasins and shorts. Sometimes I'll pocket a tank top if the course chances across a road. Mostly I stick to wild-animal-trailed boonies, scaling then glissading down slopes, scattering green knife-edged serpentine shards, stopping only long enough to drink in a view or water from the creek. Running in spurts like this, I learn to outrun asthma.

My daily runs had stopped because of bear. Shooting one must have sent a message to the others because they hadn't bothered me since, though one clawed into a neighbor's black lab miles down the mountain. For the first time in over a month I feel safe enough to lace on running moccasins but quickly learn to stay close to low-limbed, climbable trees, because as soon as Buster gets sight or scent of me he becomes an unwelcome pace-setter.

On one of those runs, a day when the porch thermometer reads ninety-seven degrees, Buster swishes away buffalo gnats in the shade of clumping juniper trees, too hot to take interest in me. Left alone I tender foot about the forested draws until thirst brings me down on all fours by the creek.

Face planted in the water I don't hear the vehicle approach. When I wipe water from my eyes I see through low boughs a rig stopped on the road across the creek. Two people, slightly stooped by age, survey the surroundings like they own them. The white crew cab they lean against, a fusion between a truck and a station wagon, is a sign they have money. Most people around here drive trucks, usually beaters, not hybrids.

If I stand up, their view will include me in all my natural glory. Fearing disclosure, my reptilian brain fires away and I slither away lowly unseen, Oregon grape leaves scraping my bare belly.

At the cabin I dress in cutoffs and a collared shirt, and then run down the road to confront these well-heeled trespassers.

The fancy rig brakes to a stop at a curve in the road just before we have a head-on. A man in a deeply crown-creased cowboy hat is behind the wheel. An orange-haired woman sits beside him and an oatmeal-colored poodle with brick red stain-rimmed eyes is perched on a beige carpeted platform between them. Their weather-beaten faces flush in surprise to see me in front of their polished grill. They step out but leave the engine running to air condition the barking poodle.

They, I learn after exchanging tentative pleasantries, were the ones responsible for tying yellow tags to my/our trees. A budget approach to establishing boundaries of forty acres they recently bought without paying for a legal survey. They were regional ranchers who planned to build a vacation home up in the piney cool of this mountain, half a mile below my cabin.

First rogue bears followed by Mr. Ed on steroids. Now, future neighbors. Trouble came in threes was the proverb I hoped not to further test.

18. Men

"Ah got a rubber. And all night." Don Paulsen leans into me and holds out a foil packet in his ranch-roughed hand to prove it.

He'd ridden Maggie all this way to see if I needed any help, at an hour when he knew I would be winding down for the day. I didn't want to seem rude or anything so I invited him inside to show off my recent fix—a piece of chink that had fallen out above the kitchen sink. As I point to the clear silicone bead rimming the repair Don nails me.

"See."

He palms the Cracker Jack-sized prize he is eager to share, the other hand pinning my shoulder to the wall.

Even with youth on my side I can't seem to leverage myself out of this predicament with an old man. I try reasoning, "What about Orinda?"

"She's at her sister's fer the night. Aside, she quit givin' me lovin' a long time ago."

I can see why. That sluice-stained, liver-lipped pucker is enough to make anyone want to take a long vacation.

Don's bristly jowls are so close I can chew the smell of snooze on his breath, as I try to figure how to protect myself from this rogue neighbor. The nearest weapons are out of reach—the fire poker hangs behind the stove, the Buck knife by the sink. With only fragile wits for defense, I fake a sneeze. Don's reflexive move to wipe spittle from his cheek allows me to jerk free and lunge for the poker.

"You better go." I jab the forked prong in his direction. Don stands his ground despite a stave of forged rebar between us.

"But ah' need my lovin' as much as you," he pleads, his eyes dewy as his mule.

"Now!" I thrust the poker closer to his belt buckle. "Or, I'm telling Orinda. And the whole town too!"

This does the trick and he rides away on Maggie, who is less of an ass than he is.

For reasons it will take me a while to register, sometimes I pique interest in people I meet. Mostly men, because they are the ones that handle my transactions in hardware store aisles or in lumber yards. During these exchanges, some, usually the older ones give me a deep twinkling crow-eyed look that holds fatherly concern and forthrightly will tell me why I should buy the more expensive galvanized nails. More often than not, the younger ones give me cocky BS. Maybe they are unsettled by a young woman wearing cutoffs and a tank top under an open flannel shirt rather than a dress. Or maybe their masculinity is threatened because I know how to use what I buy and they are not accustomed to a little woman who can wield tools, wearing whatever.

Whenever a clerk or store owner asks what I'm going to do with spikes, cement, rebar, bastard file—whatever I'm buying—I tell them it's for building. But I lie when they ask where I'm building—a white lie to discourage uninvited interests.

Although I never divulge my exact location, sometimes people trail stories that end at the cabin. One early evening I was chopping firewood when a man showed up offering his unsolicited services.

"Heard your cam shaft needed work," said that recent divorcee, who drove up with beer on his breath in a pickup bright as the drained Hamm's cans I'd later find on the road.

Before his arrival I never even knew my truck had a cam shaft. Like others, I sent this uninvited visitor back down the mountain on a road as dicey and remote as I practice being.

Yarns spinning around these parts about a young woman alone in a log cabin at the end of a wilderness road were tangled in fact and fiction. Shooting the bear inflamed curiosities and that led to more uninvited visitors. Until the bear story simmered down, I kept a new keyed Master padlock on the green gate.

I slid one note in the screen door of the judge's downtown house. I put two other notes—one in an unstamped envelope addressed to my brother and sister and one in a stamped envelope addressed to the hybrid-driving ranchers—inside the county road mailbox my siblings and I share. Each penned half-slip paper read, *Green gate key under biggest gray rock left of closest pine tree.* This is as much home security as I can score around here.

On my way back from town errands, I stop to chat with Orinda. I pull a plaid cotton shirt over my tank top before knocking. When the door opens, I'm met with a stare as icy as the bottom shelf in the chest freezer behind my neighbor.

She is "too busy to talk," she declares and the screen door bangs shut behind her.

No one on this mountain is ever too busy to talk. On the contrary, talking with neighbors is the only thing that keeps us from talking to ourselves.

Even Rhonda looks like she doesn't want to crack open the door enough for entry into mudroom, when I stop at her house to ask her if she knows "what's going on with Orinda?"

"Well," Rhonda draws out that first word long enough to make me feel ashamed of something I must be responsible for even though, standing before my closest neighbor, I'm oblivious to what it might be. "Come in. If ya don't already know I'll tell ya.'" The door slides shut behind us.

Rhonda leans against the wall, directly beneath a haloed portrait of the heavenly prophet. The print and woman look down upon me as Rhonda unravels a web of stories woven since the night Don Paulsen played Rube Goldberg with a bucket and a bell. Stories of how I invited a man to stay the night spread as fast as word about my uninvited relationship with bears. This scuttlebutt has snowballed into stories about how I entertain *men* at night. That's the story Rhonda told me.

Jesus!

"Just be careful of my brother's horse. He may charge you at the rose-hip gate," I warn Rhonda as I leave her house that afternoon. It's time to clean up the part of my reputation as a young female recluse that includes prostitution. She said she'd go to Orinda's later that day to extend my luncheon invitation which includes how to find the key hiding rock. I need to clear up any illusions that what I do on the mountain is done under a red light.

At noon, three days after extending an olive branch guised as a lunch invite, Rhonda parks the family pickup at the turn around below the cabin. She must have been able to convince Orinda that I am not a little lady of the night because she gets out of the passenger side. They are both wearing below-the-knee-length dresses. I'm wearing clean chinos, and a white Oxford shirt with a pale orange stain I hope neither woman will notice.

We sit at the white-clothed maple dinette to eat. Luncheon is spaghetti, salad and garlic bread. Dessert is Nabisco Nilla Wafers topped with peanut butter and a banana slice. With only a wood stove and a small ice chest, that's about as gourmet as it gets here.

Everything is served on my mother's gold-gilded china to make the mundane appear as refined as I would like to appear.

Rhonda points to her waist, "On a diet," she says when I offer her more spaghetti before her first serving is finished.

"Had a big breakfast," claims Orinda, who also passes on seconds.

Dessert is served on the porch steps. Rhonda nibbles a cookie then pulls out a plastic bag from her purse and begins darning a sock. Orinda seems to have warmed a bit after seeing how I live and the three of us engage in small talk.

"Want to see what I've been working on?" I ask the two ladies.

Shouldering the rifle, I feel protective as we walk down to the building site then stare into the pit.

"Honey," Orinda puts a hand on my arm and I jump because her gesture is nurturing and foreign to my touching history. "You shouldn't be working this hard. You are a woman after all."

When my neighbors leave there are lots of dirty dishes and leftovers I can't bury. As the china air dries I curl in the hammock and do something rare—relax and read in the mid-day. *Solitude* sails out of hand just as I'm dozing off with page-bound May Sarton on my chest. The book lands, open-faced above the bottom step Buster nuzzles.

Begrudgingly I unfold out of the hammock, dust off the hardback and face the horse who for the first time does not give me a Dennis-the-Menace stare, but gives me sugar eyes, something I've never before seen in that bull-headed skull. I retreat inside and return, leftovers in hand. Buster lips the wilted lettuce from my outstretched palm faster than soggy peanut butter wafers that glue to his apple-sized molars. Satiated, he snorts a nostril sigh, turns and shuffles away. I get back in the hammock, exchanging solitude for a cold bowl of spaghetti.

19. The Big Pour

Since shooting the bear, I'd not encountered or been bothered by one. Building a bear-proof enclosure no longer seems driven by necessity. But I stockpiled three truckloads of ninety-four-pound Portland cement sacks covered with Visqueen. Neighboring, yards of three-quarter ag and washed sand also waited to be mixed and poured into footings and walls I had absolutely no inkling how to configure. If it wasn't mixed before winter and spring soaked in it would be like throwing away good money. Penny-pinching had gotten me this far so I set out to finish what I started.

Constructing and pouring footings I could do on my own. But building and filling forms tall as me, was beyond my reach. I scraped my savings to pay Jim for the skills and muscle I lacked. I also knew he had another job, building a mansion-style log cabin for those hybrid-driving ranchers half a mile below my bear-proof studio site and was being paid a good living wage by people who provided power tools to build by code. So, I was greatly appreciative when he said he could spare time to work with me.

It takes us nearly two full days of scraping loaned boards together to re-construct the footing forms I made, spaced twelve inches apart and stabilized with rebar spikes. Though we haven't collaborated together on anything major since the cabin, cobbling silliness into the serious mix of measuring and pounding is proof we haven't rusted our connection.

Midway into the second day I hand Jim a shovel. "Let's pretend they are dug-out canoes," I say, pointing to the footings we've nailed together from scrap wood.

I wedge inside one of four forms that will be used to set concrete and not my silly ass. Jim sits atop another, his legs bent and draping over the sides of one-by-fours hammered to the lengths of boa constrictor coffins. Using my shovel like a paddle I J-stroke wide so as not to collide starboard with Jim who, playing along, is also paddling in pine-needle rapids.

By the time we quit splashing around in earthbound wakes and begin to use those shovels rightfully again, this impromptu land-locked paddle has cost me five bucks. Well worth the added expenditure, I reason, because playfulness seasons the monotony of manual labor.

There is no fooling around when it comes time to fill those forms. By the end of the second day, boards that only hours before floated freely along with our imaginations are topped off with cement hoed creamy. They haven't begun to set when Don Paulsen shows up, all amnesia-like about the night he packed up a rubber.

"Gotta spit into em," he says while wedging a juicy plug in his cheek. He leans over the footing I'm smooth finishing with a trowel. "Fer good luck."

Fresh sluice coils out between his teeth and a stream lands slickly in the wet cement. "Here ya go." Don holds out his tobacco tin which I refuse out of past experience. Instead I pooty-tooty my piece of pink Bazoka gum by now as flavorful as a shoe sole. Jim refuses to spit.

Two days later the footings are cured and I whack off the form boards, then pull out nails and scrape away dried cement. These are reused for wall forms, which takes Jim and me four full days to build. It takes another two days to wire together a framework of rebar. These are lowered into and anchored to the footings.

The time Jim budgets to work with me more than doubles. I dip deeper into my savings, financing a bear-proof cellar—an investment in my future on this mountain, I hope.

I'm halfway to the gravel pit for another yard of washed sand when I realize my wallet is on a windowsill in the cabin instead of my back pocket. I always paid my bills in full and was about to turn back but remembered my hidden booty.

One time when I was settling my tab with Emery, he gave some advice while handing back wilted change, "I know fishermen and loggers who keep money in their boots for emergencies."

I wondered why Emery would tell me this as his occupation kept him tied to a cash register from dawn to dusk, but after pocketing dollar bills and silver change I went to the bank and withdrew a one- hundred-dollar bill. After folding it in half and slipping it under the insole of my work boot I forgot about it. Until this financial crunch.

My loaded truck idles next to Janette's booth while she waits for payment. I hoist my foot onto the seat, unstring the upper eyelets, pull off my left boot and uncover a treasure trove of pulverized grime. On to the right boot. Beneath the leather insole, pasted down by gravity and sweat, I discover my one hundred dollar bill—worn in half at the crease and plain useless now.

With the promise of returning soon I drive to the bank, loaded down with unpaid sand, sad money and sadder story which I present to the bank the teller. After some behind the counter conferencing with higher-ups the teller returns and tells me that if the pieces meet and the entire bill is intact she can exchange the damaged bill for an unspoiled one.

As she holds the halves to the light, I hold my breath. She aligns the ends on the counter like two pieces of a puzzle mating. On the other side of the counter I exhale, relieved when she hands me a crisp new one hundred dollar bill that I immediately exchange for five twenties. Back at the gravel yard, Janette puts one in her cash box before handing me change and a receipt.

Originally, I planned to mix all the cement in a wheelbarrow.

According to Jim, we would not.

"You're a damn fool if you think we can mix it all by hand," he said and proceeded to point out the labor and time-saving benefits of powering up a gas generator to turn the mixer as well as running a pump rather than hauling water up from the creek bucket by bucket.

Paying Jim to help me build a foundation was necessary. But renting a generator and mixer to do the work we could manage between us, seemed an exorbitant and unnecessary drain on my limited financial resources.

At this age I banked more bullheaded determination than I did discretionary income. Thankfully the treasure buried in my boot will cover this unplanned rental equipment.

The generator drones, burrs and coughs and chokes out dead when it needs gas. The hose is left running down slope when not in use. We take turns shoveling cement, sand and ag into the mixer. Whoever isn't tending mixing cement is loading it into a wheelbarrow and balancing it downhill. Twice a rock twists my grip and I end up on the ground with a wet load, only myself worth salvaging.

The first day we fill two wall forms. After Jim leaves I hose off the tools, the mixer and refuel the generator so everything is ready in the morning.

The next day, we work again from 8 a.m. to 4 p.m. Early that afternoon Don Paulsen shows up again, offering more superstition rather than a hand.

"Gotta put something in those walls so they remember who built em." He says as I shovel cement into one form.

Before Don arrived I'd no idea cement walls held memories, but follow suit and drop in a chewing gum wrapper next to Don's tobacco tin. Jim adds a pine cone and we cement over our offerings.

Late that afternoon Jim tows away a tired cement mixer and an overheated generator. Motorized equipment I would have gladly sacrificed a fresh one-hundred-dollar bill to create walls with consciousness.

20. The Moon and I

In the last few days I've mixed and poured enough cement to impress the Hoover Dam masons.

Repetitive manual labor that beefed up my forefathers' fore arms has also tempered my obliques taut as purse strings, cinching my celestially-dictated reproductive pockets. In other words, my ovaries feel like tennis balls volleyed between top-seeded rivals; my uterus is their warm-up backboard.

On top of all the predictable pains associated with mixing and moving an ocean of cement my *friend* has arrived. When I was building the cabin, my friend took a hike with secondary amenorrhea. When she decided to return, she arrived hand in hand with regular but excruciating, debilitating menstrual cramps. Now, this unwelcome womb mate is settling in for a stay to remind me that, yes, I can work hard as a man but still must contend with my fragile, female plumbing.

In the evening after the last eight-hour day of filling forms, I lie in the hammock, well past dark, drinking the Boone's Farm Shelly left behind. I've been saving it to share with a bona fide friend who never visits. By dark the bottle is empty and my cramping friend, merely nullified by cheap wine, parties on.

Groggily, clutching my gut, I haul myself up into the loft, wrap in sheets printed with a cartoon bird; the only thing remotely funny in a night I spend curled around bloody pangs sharp as a freshly filed chisel. The cramps rage on into the morning and I begin taking two Motrin every four hours throughout a day I spend in the hammock. Strung out on the porch, I draw a deer skull I found on a hike. Long before weathered white, even bone-eating beetles had lost their appetite for it. I added the skull to my collection of drawing objects stored in a restored slat wood crate.

The skull is positioned on the upended side of the box so it is at eye level and I don't have to raise my own too much to see the bone head. Late that afternoon it begins to rain, a needed diversion as I am identifying too much with what I draw. I replace the skull inside the crate and take my cramps indoors.

By late afternoon it is dark enough outside to justify lighting a lamp inside. Wind gusts drive wet sheets sideways onto the porch, soaking the hammock. I stare at the flaming wick, worry rain will hamper the cellar walls curing and nosh down the end half of a package of Keebler shortbreads, running a finger inside the wrapping when the last cookie is eaten. I feel even emptier when the lone remaining crumb is sucked clean off my tweezed thumb and wish small elves would appear to bake a big fresh batch of uncommonly good cookies—an apparition as depleted as the Motrin and wine bottles.

The second rainy day is as stimulating as the first was. I read, write and draw; reverse the order, draw, write, read, then stare at the limp hammock outside on the porch to keep from thinking about how the rain could also be soaking through the form boards.

The hunger is gnawing above my agonized abdomen. Since the bears had their way I've not replaced my grain and legume survival stores. Two cans of Green Giant French-cut green beans, one can of tuna and a package of saltines are the only edibles in store. Fresh supplies are only thirteen miles away, but the mountain road runs with mud so slick even the nimble Datsun couldn't make it past the rose-hip gate. I know this as fact. The little truck remains stuck in mud from an aborted escape attempt on rainy day number two.

On the third day rain turns to drizzle and my hopes rise then sink again in the afternoon when the sky lobs water balloons. My food supply has gone the way of prescription pain meds and rot gut which only tamed the cramps to a dull ache. My soul for cookies, a bottle of wine! Anything to punctuate the boredom of being stuck in my own numb head.

I could hike down in conditions that have turned Shit and Slide and the Eliminator into the Nile River and drive Tank to town, from where it is parked in the judge's meadow. Hoofing down the muddy road is possible. But driving Tank back up would only end in the same calamity that claimed the Datsun. Plus, everything I've ingested to nullify my friend has made my legs wobbly.

At this point it is safer to starve than to set out shakily in search of food. Breakfast, lunch and dinner that day are the same; a mix of tuna and crackers, kept chilled in the creek and rationed out in five-hour increments. My mood and my belly contrary to a gang of happy little elves.

By early evening of that third rained-in day showers have relented and so has my pain. I feel strong enough to go on a short painting trip. I pull on a thick wool shirt, shoulder the French easel and hike across the creek to my favorite old juniper.

Storm clouds scud overhead like bumper cars wheeled by drunken winds. Safe and sheltered from this mayhem, under ancient boughs, I paint until the slight drizzle becomes raindrops again. By the time I've packed up the easel it is pouring.

Rain mottles the painstakingly blended sky even as I shield the canvas against my thigh. I no longer pack the cumbersome rifle; it stays in the truck. Boo-Boo hangs from my belt leaving one hand free to carry the painting, the other for bushwhacking and balancing on a log across the creek.

Back at the cabin I leave the easel on the porch, bring the painting inside to dry, stoke the fire, stare out the window and watch the clouds part and the moon rise. My hollow, growling gut reminds me it is the only full thing around. There is only sleep to fill me. I wash my hands of the evening's work and crawl up into the loft to consume it.

When I first moved into this cabin, insomnia which I'd never known before visited me, welcome as a bedfellow who kicks and snores. On sleepless nights when it was out I charted the moon's arc through the three loft windows until it sank in the West and the East fired red.

Tonight, full moon light saturates the loft, insomnia snuggles in, and I kick back.

I climb down from the loft and unfold the easel under the shelter of the porch. The moon above the pines is perfect as a vanilla Necco Wafer I would stand on my tippy toes to lick: so perfectly round that if I painted it exactly as it appeared, it would look like it belonged inked in a newspaper cartoon strip.

Squeezing paint onto a palette I mix values, the smell of linseed oil in my paint cup and tuna on my breath. As I mound Prussian Blue tones, I feel something stir inside me and it isn't menstrual throbbing. A crystal-clear energy rounds my belly, visceral motion I don't want to stop, kind of like being on a roller coaster but without feeling car sick.

I set my brushes on the easel, walk down the steps, stand on the hillside and raise my hands. My shirt too, hikes up, exposing my navel to the moon—my solar plexus the bull's-eye of lunar light. Hands over head, feeling the planetary pull, I must drop to my hands and knees, because there is no shrubbery within reach to anchor me to an earth I am not yet ready to leave. Hollowed out by hunger, I am a conduit. The lunar attraction strong enough to pull me off my feet is either a freak mystical exchange or an indicator that I need a solid meal pretty quick.

By morning the rain has stopped, the sun is out and while I wait for the road to soak up I hand-saw two, twenty-four-inch circles of quarter-inch Masonite then stretch and gesso pieces of an old cotton sheet over each. I'd been drawing in circles, now I decided to paint inside of them.

Jamming twigs and branches under the tires, gunning it back and forth, I free the truck then head to town.

It's dusk by the time I drive back and park in the judge's meadow. With Yogi resting beside a pre-set palette, I eat cheese and crackers on the tailgate and wait. The pine-tipped mountain ridge threatens to poke a hole in the moon as it rises up bright enough for me to discern the palette's values of Prussian Blue, burnt sienna and white. Bright enough to fill two circles with moonlit forest silhouettes I sleep like a log that night.

In the morning, critiquing these paintings I conclude they are trite. By my second cup of coffee, I'm still wondering why I didn't find success overnight—the compositions look like pages from a children's coloring book.

When are you going to stop fooling around and start to paint? I chide myself, sulk, give in to my ineptitude and accept the fact I'm a half-baked neophyte in just about whatever I do.

I take another sip of coffee, then answer myself. *I am not fooling around. It's just that I'm painting from the inside out where there is more than meets the eye.*

21. Neighborly Advice

One afternoon I stop by the Taynton's house for a quick visit. From her recliner, Anabell sees me through the screen door. "Let yer self in Lavon!" and she relaxes back into a well-seasoned Naugahyde recliner.

I sit beside her on the couch, the plastic coverlet crinkling and sticking to the backs of my bare legs.

Anabell asks what I've been up to and does not turn down the volume so I must make myself heard over the TV. I fill her in about the details of building and pouring footings and walls but say nothing of my recent moon exchange, fearing she will offer me one of her usual home remedies like Walla-Walla onion and cheddar cheese as a cure-all for sleeplessness.

"Need any help Lavon?" she asks after I tell her that I'm ready to pull apart the forms.

"Nah. I'm fine. It's just nails," I say, then stay and watch the tail end of *As the World Turns* over a bowl of Neapolitan ice cream. Anabell overweighs my dish with strawberry. "My favorite," she says, filling her bowl with chocolate and vanilla. Although I prefer chocolate and vanilla, I keep my mouth shut around a spoonful of selfless consideration.

The day after my visit with Anabell, I set out to dismantle the forms. Rain has soaked the boards but didn't touch the cement. As the damp morning evaporates into a sunny afternoon the boards dry, clenching those sixteen-penny's tighter.

The nails shriek, *let us be!* Even more defiantly when a crowbar pulls each screaming head out. I take to calling them little suckers and more, as I wrench my wrist back and forth, jerking and twisting one way then the other before a nail pulls free and falls to rust away amid a pine needle potpourri.

While I yell at nails and they scream back, Del and Anabell show up unexpectedly. It is the middle of the week so Del has quit his work, most likely because Anabell told him about mine.

With two more sets of hands helping, form boards peel away easily, leaving grainy impressions in four damp cement walls. By late afternoon the last board has been de-nailed, scraped clean, and stacked for Jim's friend Jake to pick up. I'm ready to call it a day, but Anabell and Del stay, insisting on helping me straighten all the nails we've pulled out.

"Ya can re-use em," Del says, a steely bouquet of twisted sixteens in his fist. Got anything to put them in?"

I do.

We scour the building site filling a dented and punctured two-gallon bucket with dejected nails then dump it between us. Anabell grabs a bunch, sits down on a log and starts hammering away. Del and I join her.

"This one looks too far gone," I hold out a nail bent like a horseshoe, the formation we make, sitting on windfalls and stumps.

"Give it ta me." Anabell takes the nail, places it on a log and in one sound blow nearly straightens it.

We chat away, smacking nails in positions they weren't manufactured to be hammered, until most have been resurrected nearly straight and dropped into a holey bucket.

After Del and Anabell leave, I stow the recycled sixteen-penny's beside a box of shiny new ones. Before today I had no idea nails could be recycled, because I'd never been in a position to use up all the use in something useful.

I am out running the afternoon Jake hauled away clean form boards and stop when I see the judge in a gathering of apple trees growing at the base of his grassy meadow. He explains that he is propping up a branch a bear broke earlier that week.

"They have a sweet tooth same as you and me. Hand me that board will ya, Sqeedunk," the judge says addressing me with his peculiar brand of nickname.

I pass him a splintery two-by-four and he nails it to the framework.

"They eat so many apples it makes em' drunk."

"What?" I steady the board as the judge wedges the top to support the limb he hopes will grow stout again.

"When they get a belly full of apples, especially on a hot day, they go and lie down in the sun for a nap. The apples ferment in their gut, makes em' drunk."

"Really?" I think the judge is pulling my leg.

"Really." He climbs down to nail a jury-rigged brace. "And they crap piles big as a pie." Apples shake on the branches the judge reinforces along with my new gastronomic image.

Later that week, when I was out running bareback on trails, I came across a specimen not pictured in my scatology reference. The book mentioned the change of season is evident in wild animal poo. The author didn't use that exact terminology but did indicate that, especially in late summer, omnivores fill up on ripe berries and fruit which alters the color and texture of their excrement.

A bear hunter also told me that late summer was the best time to kill a bear for eating because all the seasonal fruit and berries sweetened their meat. Later, that hunter would be cited for using rancid bacon to bait and kill bears out of season.

The shit that tripped my running pace appeared to be more of an aborted apple kugel than animal excreta. I squatted for a closer look. Prodded the pile with a pine stick, felt the hot sun on my neck, and a chill run up my spine, as I realized a pair of moccasins was my sole defense against what I could never out run.

I knew then the judge wasn't pulling my leg and the bear baiter didn't lie. Chock through with red, brown and yellow apple skins, seeds and stems, this poop pile would more than fill a pie pan and it was glistening fresh. I kept running.

Time was also running out if I was going to be in Northern California to resume my art education. Before leaving I wanted to fell enough trees for wall logs. There was no time to drawknife them but the bark would protect the cambium until I returned to further the creation of what I would leave a half-baked, bear-proof studio.

Jim felled sixteen trees the last day he was here. So that was a start. It took me three days to fell and limb what I guessed would be enough to buck into logs I could wrangle into a finished structure.

I didn't want to leave seventy trees lying on wet, freezing and thawing ground over winter and spring. I also didn't want to ask the Nelsons to Cat them out because they refused payment. Nor did I want the site carved up by heavy equipment and sought out a means of dragging and decking with less environmental impact.

A small ad for Mule Logging was printed in The Juniper Press, a free weekly mimeographed newsletter distributed throughout town. I picked up a copy from the checker's counter then dialed the number for an advertised listing at the pay phone outside of Chester's. As it rang, I scanned the community bulletin board—plenty of listings for hay, some Australian Shepherd puppies, a garage sale on Cozart Street that ended last week and nothing posted under the Lost and Found column. By the time I pictured one of those puppies in my lap the ringing stopped.

A voice on the other end of the line, shaky and graveled at first, grew assured and easy as Rick Higgins professed he had been logging with mules for over forty years. "Hell," he added, "I been workin' in the woods so long I shit logs."

I didn't further that part of our conversation, but I did agree to pay him ten dollars an hour to drag and deck my logs. Two days later I met the man and his mules.

Rick Higgins didn't look like the big man he sounded like over the pay phone. At sixty-seven he had a mattress of thick white hair and carried himself like a brick. He'd trailered two mules and parked his rig in a wide spot below the cabin.

"Don't want to harness them until we actually start ta workin'" he explains as he introduces me to Oranges and Pickles.

At the end of the day when those mules are unharnessed they have dragged seventy logs up above the building site. Rick never used a harsh word or laid a hand on either animal. He controlled them with sugar cubes instead.

The next morning I said goodbye to that log deck and a cement-walled five-foot deep hole and drove to Northern California. I locked the cabin door, the key beside a rib bone in my pocket.

22. Summer Break

At the end of May, after nine months of studio classes, I pack my belongings into plastic milk crates that doubled as bookshelves in the Mendocino apartment. Along with my drawing table, these hampers fill the back of the Datsun. If only my past, present and future could be as manageably contained I'd be one happy camper.

On May thirty-first, I nest Inipi in my well-worn green cotton hat on the bench seat and head for another summer at the cabin. Coiled inside, snug as a bug, my cat-in-a-hat mews as we leave the saliferous coastal airs that late afternoon, drive through redwood spires, and call it a night amid alkaline flats.

Scuffling about in the headlights, I clear twigs and rocks to prepare for a roadside rest. By the time I have unpacked, Inipi is wide awake inside the cab, and playfully pouncing between the dash and the floorboard housing water and kibble saucers and a shoe box filled with sand. I lock the cab and prepare for my own nocturnal play.

I unroll the sleeping bag beside the truck while passing headlights fracture a cutting desert night. Boo-Boo is loaded, cocked, safety off—my only defense against any full-bladdered psycho who might stumble upon more than a spot of relief behind the brambly Manzanita screening the Datsun.

Upright inside the sleeping bag, I draw, aim and practice being threatening.

"I shoot first...ask questions later." I repeat this until tired out by all my bluffing, and lay Boo-Boo beside a makeshift pillow. A doe-colored ski jacket, once relegated for that purpose only, cradles my head. Instead of dreaming about the mogluled slopes of Vail, Snowmass, Steamboat and Alta that I skied as a young teen, I think about how to make it through a night adjusting my bones over alluvium soil. Before closing my eyes I rise on an elbow, give the flatland a final flashlight sweep and spotlight a scorpion scuttling by. I repeat, "I shoot first...ask questions later," just to hear how convincing I might sound to anything big enough and near enough to trigger my half-cocked reflexes.

More disturbing to me than close proximity to a venomous arachnid is a memory that rises up as soon as I lie down. It was a dream I'd had years ago, in Clyde Holliday State Park the night before I met a realtor in a cowboy hat. A nightmare with blood streaming through my fine long hair.

As I adjust to a rocky roadside I muse my dream was really a premonition of what would actually transpire, another time, to others in a park northeast of where I roadside camp.

Two college girls on summer break, zipped inside their tent in Cline Falls State Park were assaulted by a man dressed as a young cowboy. He drove his truck over their tent then repeatedly whacked them with a hatchet, leaving them hacked bloody, broken, hanging to life by severed threads. Their attacker was never caught.

Which means that man and men like him are still out there.

Which means what happened to those girls could happen to this girl.

If there was still life left in me, after a savage encounter, it would be a long crawl for help at this time of night on a desolate roadside. If I died from injuries—at this point pre-imagined—I didn't know how long Inipi would last, locked in the cab until my body was found and the cat in the hat was rescued.

I will myself to stay awake for both our sakes and worry Boo-Boo's trigger like a rosary bead stuck between a prayer.

At dawn, puffy-eyed and stiff, I rise from ground that I found limited rest upon. In early morning light I empty Boo-Boo's chamber and re-holster the gun before fashioning a makeshift pet harness from the belt of my ski-jacket pillow. Hitched to the bumper, Inipi doesn't strain against this improvised brace attached to twenty feet of twine as I shake morning dew off the sleeping bag and check for scorpions.

After prying back the top of a tuna can with my Swiss Army knife opener, I dust off a twig and fork some into Inipi's bowl. He licks into moist fish flakes as I wash my face with water stowed for this purpose only. By sunrise I am fresh as the day rising and Inipi's belly balloons with breakfast.

The sleeping bag is stuffed and stowed beside leftover canned tuna in the truck bed.

The last leg of the drive between Lakeview and John Day is predictably direct except for pit stops to express my roadside culinary idiocy. Every minute behind the wheel I'm sure I'm going to die and wishing I'd never eaten tuna remaining in a can hours after the lid was hinged open on a day that climbed into the nineties. By the time I face the Eliminator, the last leg to the cabin, I figure being run over by a truck and bladed up is preferable to suffering from ptomaine poisoning.

That first night back at the cabin, I hydrate by guzzling down nearly a six-pack of green glass 7 Up bottles specially purchased at Chester's. On the third day, still feeling effects of food poisoning, I go to town to buy more soda and to find my truck. While in Mendocino I sold the Gremlin at great sentimental loss, but I could not afford the upkeep of a vehicle that couldn't make the grade. Now I was down to two vehicles, a papa and a mama or a mama and a baby depending on how one measured the scale of a nurturing truck.

Before turning off Main Street I glance over at Emery's Bakery Café and discover those very words scraped off the storefront window. I park and go inside where a waitress in a sea-green uniform tells me Emery retired. That's all she knew or would say.

Proceeding to Dan Gray's I discover my big truck, like Emery, also mysteriously missing. The space where it is usually parked under a cottonwood tree is as vacant as Dan's house appears—not even a curtain in the living room window.

"Moved," is the only explanation my neighbor Glen Nelson gives later that afternoon when I ask, "What happened to Dan Gray?"

Through letters I'd kept in touch with the Nelsons, Jim, Anabell and Del. I also subscribed to The Blue Mountain Eagle, the newspaper arriving in my Mendocino post office box, a week after it hit the stands in John Day. Not one issue published a column inch on Emery retiring or the vanishing of Dan Gray and that faded green truck.

I lean against the ridge-barked cottonwood, feeling angry but a tad relieved—that payload of upkeep was out of my life. With that three-quarter ton of fun gone, I was down to one truck. Tank's ability to haul was the only reason I would miss that heap. As the cottonwood fluffs mix in sneezy breezes I think about the precarious friendship of two men who, like that old Ford, I will probably never see again.

A few days is enough to dilute post-ptomaine poisoning lethargy. I feel well enough to unpack the Datsun, starting with the cab. Bending to lift Inipi's traveling litter box I'm startled by squealing between the floorboard and stick-shift flange.

Though not even in gear, that manual transmission is throttling with a life of its own. A whispering, high-pitched staccato is emanating under the rubber boot—the sun-hardened seal crazed and peeling. I drape myself over the driver's side of the bench seat, stretch out and pry up a corner of that diaphragm, then peek into a space where the sun never shines, a place I'd never once explored in my limited maintenance of the Datsun.

Aiming a flashlight, I spot a writhing mass of baby mice. Each one is half the size of my pinkie and I have small hands that are nevertheless big enough to handle the fate born inside the gearbox. They seem abandoned and, as no matronly mouse appears to thwart the hand of their discoverer, I assume care of these orphans.

Like me these babies had been left to fend for themselves. Without a nurturing paw to guide them, they would surely starve. If set free they would be victims of exposure. If left in the gear box they'd be throttled to mousey cream.

Pinching my thumb and forefinger like tweezers, I prize out all eight of these squeakers, one by one. Squiggling away they would have blinked in sudden sunlight if their pinhole eyes were open. With tender care I lower each pink pod into a green cotton hat that most recently cradled a Siamese cat. Marveling at the wriggling minutiae below the brim, I plod up to the cabin, every step of the way planning a farewell party for these foundlings. At any point, I could upturn the hat and release them into an unruly patch of forest where they would end up as appetizers. Yet I, as their self-proclaimed guardian, will not allow those visionless nippers to be eaten alive by an owl or coyote or suffer further the consequences of nurturing neglect.

On the porch I set the hat in the shade on the work bench to protect these newborns from crisping in full sun. They ball into a collective fist, squirming like fat maggots, emitting singular squeals that rise to group cry as I fill a Mason jar nearly to the brim with water poured from my drinking bucket.

"Bye, bye babies," I say as swiftly as I fold the hat and funnel out every one into the jar's open mouth. Then screw the lid down fast. And tight.

Shocked by the splash and imminent death, these blind mice dog-paddle for existence, sucking up a slice of air calculated to absorb the placement of their furless bodies. For less than twenty seconds, a fresh spurt of life surges through their blushing, translucent flesh—the instinctive, automatic response to drowning. Appearing more like canned tangerine sections than mini-mammals, they scramble for survival as clearly futile and slippery as the glass wall entombing them.

There is still time. I could open that jar and pour the spongy litter to dry ground. But I wait until each baby floats belly-up to form a jetsam wreath of waterlogged waifs and pious humanely intent. Drowning, I rationalize, is easier than fathoming abandonment.

I do not bury those breathless babies. Do not even thread together a twig cross to mark their passing. I lined their soggy bodies in a straight row like I'd seen human bodies pictured in history books noting heinous, heinous crimes. Sheltered under the twisted boughs of a bull pine I knew the open air mass grave would be departed by morning. Fresh coyote scat nearby the bull pine that a Great Horned Owl perched in every night was sure sign those fresh dead mice would end up as a late night snack. Though I wasn't sure if owls favored carrion.

That night I dream about those newly-dead newborns, fierce-eyed and big as black bears in my subconscious state. They numbered in the amount I'd drowned and were everywhere—hovering above ground where they no longer rested. Each and every mouse spirit lingered in the pines, waiting to get me.

In my dream I could not step off the porch for fear that one or two or the whole damn ghost litter would grab me by the ankles, drag me into the creek, then sit on me—my last breath, water, like theirs had been.

Attila the Hun, Hitler, Idi Amin…oh, the list can go on. And on.

That afternoon I added my name to the role of imbecilic despots who get away with murder. But I hadn't killed for pleasure, power or revenge. Or out of self-defense. Or hatching psychosis.

I killed out of projection. If I'd let those baby mice live on, their lives would have been motherless torment.

23. Coming Clean

Unlike the baby mice, the log deck above the building site could not be put to rest. Late last summer mules and a man helped me drag and pile them and now it was up to me to buck them into manageable eighteen-footers, and drawknife them after winter pulled their bark tight as glued-on girdles.

I hadn't really used the drawknife since building the cabin and locate it precisely where I'd last left it, hanging from a nail alongside axes and hatchets beneath the porch. The handle is black with old pitch and the blade still razor-edge sharp from its last file and whetstone visit.

The morning after the Mason jar massacre, drawknife in hand, I look down on that log jam. Nearly a hundred trees, three or four times my length, each outweighing me thrice or more. Viewed as a whole, whittling that pile into skinned logs seems as impracticable as sucking life from a slice of air. Instead of succumbing to this choring magnitude I break the task into manageable units, one log at a time. It is one job to pull a drawknife through corky hull. Another to lift and roll a tree with an eight to twelve-inch butt then repeat the sinew-straining process and scale away until there is no bark left.

That hefty dose of food poisoning is still chipping my usual vitality. But the greatest gap in my strength is attributed to atrophy developed during months spent in coastal California studios. Just the elemental tasks required to live at the cabin—sawing, splitting wood, hauling water buckets—calls to attention sinews slackened by months of toggling switches and twisting faucets.

By late afternoon three gleaming logs have tallied into trembling forearms, back strain and pitch webbed fingers. A good soak would soothe muscle misery but, like building a bear-proof cellar studio, the thought of a hot bath is easier than the manifestation of it.

The tub is in the same place where it was leveled last summer. Blocked up over a shallow pit on four cinder blocks, it is filled with needles, leaves, scummy water and detritus-thriving microscopic parasites; a cold primordial soup I ladle out with a dented aluminum saucepan before scouring the cast iron inside white with powdery blue Comet.

Sides all gleamy, I fill the tub bucket by bucket and light a fire under it. As the water heats I prepare my toilet, balancing a bottle of Johnson's Baby Shampoo on a flat rock alongside a washcloth and brand-new Castile Soap cake. Just as I am disrobing, I hear a familiar, and at this time and place, an unwelcome bray.

Don Paulsen trots up the path on his mule Maggie as I zip up the fly on my cutoffs. If he'd arrived a minute later, I'd be butt naked and bathing.

"Howdy Lavon!" Don is fast out of the saddle. Ranch work has lubricated his joints rather than broken them down like other men his age. He prolongs his greeting by pulling me in for a hug and a kiss on the cheek, like he never learned a lesson.

I push away his brown rimmed lips slick with chew, a wad packed in his cheek, and we exchange news as Maggie stands passively, blinking in the bath-fire smoke. Through the sparse neighbor grapevine of a judge and a family of Mormons, Don heard I was back. I ask if he knew why Emery's closed. "Don't know. I never ate at his place. Orinda's a better cook than any. Why pay for what I can get free at home?" And I wish he'd go there because twilight is inching in and bats are pinging overhead. His visit finally ended with Don saying over his shoulder as he rode away, "Next time yer going to town stop on by and see Orinda."

It is nearly dark by the time I am toweling off. The bath fire is doused dead out and my skin is as fleshy pink as some baby mice I'd recently drowned. With clean wet hair dripping down my back and Inipi in my lap, I assume my Thinker pose in the rocker. By the time my mane is dry and sheeny brushed I've thought long enough and decided—before I put any more time into building a bear-proof studio I need to build a man-proof bathhouse.

When I bought my property, the lowland bordering the graveled county road was an unblemished steppe of sagebrush and juniper. After the cabin was built, houses started to pop up like tumbleweeds stopped mid-roll. Centenarian junipers were felled and left to wizen, their limbs like the skeletal remains of cattle who lapped alkaline waters. Now fresh lumber stacks mark the spots of new home sites in this high-desert prairie.

Free is spray-painted on a board leaning against a stack of plywood scrap in front of one home under construction. There are pieces in that pile big enough, I figure, to puzzle together a little bathhouse.

Rummaging through it I select as many freshly-sawn plywood squares and rectangles as can wedge compactly into the camper, the hatch left open for the boards to stick out. I'm sorry to leave more substantial lengths and widths behind, knowing Tank could have handled a load the Datsun can only toy with. Then I make good on my promise to Don and stop to visit his wife.

Orinda tiptoes through an obstacle course of free-range fowl and goats. A galvanized bucket in each hand, she does not wave back as I park in the shadow slant of their barn. Dressed in her usual razor-creased pastel blouse and slacks, a bun wound in her white hair, eyes ball-bearing steely, she continues to remind me she is the reverse of her rotund free-ranging husband.

"Afternoon Lavon." She nods as I meet her pace, three goats imprinting her every step toward the house. "Get the door for me."

I open it wide and Orinda enters sideways, buckets in hand.

"Let yourself in," she says before setting the buckets on the kitchen counter.

The screen door slams behind me and I watch Orinda fill empty Folgers Coffee cans with goat milk.

"Want some?" She folds wax paper over the tops of four cans, stretching rubber bands around the rim.

Unless it was really chilled, I didn't much care for goat milk but don't want to chance offending Orinda by refusing, so I accept the two cans she offers. It's not the first and I'm sure it won't be the last time I'll walk away with bounty from that kitchen.

When she isn't there cooking, canning, wrapping and freezing meat or washing up Orinda was outside bartering with goats and chickens. Like Rhonda, my only other woman neighbor, I've come to rely on Orinda as a mother hen to this little lost chick.

Orinda, like Rhonda, does things with her hands that mine have never taken a stab at, like hooking strips of threadbare shirts and skirts into a rag rug, aiming a teat long enough to fill a bucket and wringing a rooster's neck then plucking it. Neither woman has experienced formal education beyond high school or much travel beyond Boise or Baker. And when I'd first met them, I judged each woman as being simple. And they were. Simply good women. They cared about and were always there for me. That's more than I had with my own family so I became a straggling member of theirs.

As we each carry a full coffee can to my truck, Orinda sees the boards sticking out of the camper shell and asks, "Lavon, what are you going to do with those?"

"Build a bathhouse.—To keep the wind and rain off me when I bathe," I quickly explain, not adding that the idea is motivated by her husband's unexpected evening visits.

She already knew all about the tub. The summer before she'd helped Don load it onto the mule-drawn wagon. But she had not seen where it was located and I believe she was also clueless as to the destination of her husband's evening mule rides.

I lodge the coffee cans between my pack and the floorboard, stabilizing them for the rocky road ahead. As I turn to get behind the wheel, Orinda says, "Wait," then runs a boney hand down a pant seam, looks over her shoulder, "Follow me."

Like a fourth milk goat, I trot behind Orinda and halt when she stops in the barn. Sunlight streams through cracks in the siding, backlighting every dust, hay and dried manure mote. The goats nuzzle into a junk pile Orinda rummages through. She pulls and casts aside a history of ranching implements to reveal two rusty barrels.

"You can have them if you want," she points to the fifty-five-gallon drums welded horizontally together then raps the bottom tank. The sound rings hollow, drawing one goat near. "Get!" she commands and the goat backs into a mess of hitches and handled tools.

If I wanted the contraption my neighbor offered I didn't know it then. Mainly because I thought it was a still and wondered why it was in Orinda's possession—she being a teetotaler with a capital T—until she explains.

"When our kids were young," she forms the beginning of a smile, "We used this to heat water."

That smile softens her expression as she remembers a time where smiling must have been a regular feature of a face now forged by times tough enough to rust metal.

Orinda points to a bung hole and explains how one end of a hose was set in a body of running water like a "Crick or irrigation ditch." The other end ran into the top barrel. When the upper was filled, a fire was built in the bottom and the water got "Hot enough to boil the skin off a pig." Orinda discloses this without a hint of sentiment, making me pause to imagine the full history of this ensemble.

I bend down to open a little fire door welded to the bottom tank. Nothing inside now but the acrid tang of ashes. Orinda kneels beside me and turns a spigot welded to a pipe leading down from the upper barrel. "A hose screwed here," she points to the tarnished faucet, "drained the hot water."

Brushing hay from her slacks she stands then rummages through the junk pile, pulling out a stiff, dusty coral-rose-colored rubber hose. "Here," she hands me the uncoiled length, "This will get you started."

Two days after this introduction to a double-barrel, wood-burning hot water heater, Orinda arrives at the cabin with Don. The three of us manage to unload the stove from their truck bed. Maggie, who'd been tied to the bumper on the slow drive up the mountain, is re-hitched to a jury-rigged snow tire chain harness hooked around the barrels. The three of us cajole docile Maggie as she drags them sideways down a path too narrow for the truck to drive.

Don and I level the barrels on a welded steel cradle set firmly on a flat spot forty feet down from the creek. Orinda, Maggie's reins in hand, watches us work, her perpetually prim lips never relaxing to more than a slit. There is a little spark in her eyes though. Something I'd seen ignite when she first introduced me to this heating apparatus. I wanted to believe it was because she had a loving recollection of those drums now in my possession. Not because there was new clear space in the barn.

By late afternoon our work is complete. I offer to pay for the stove, the cradle, but Orinda shakes her head no, refusing even gas money. Don hitches Maggie back to the truck bumper and they drive down the mountain so slowly even the dust stays settled.

After they round the bend I stand on the porch and look down on the contraption. Throw in a couple of copper coils and some crockery jugs and that open-air bathroom would be Snuffy Smith complete.

The three-sided lean-to I'd planned to build to shelter the bathtub had, with the addition of those barrels, become obsolete. Now, I would need to build something much wider and taller. This would require more than scrap wood. I needed eight-foot two-by-fours and some one-by and knew where to find them.

Since returning for the summer I hadn't seen hide nor hair of my brother or Buster his colossal cojoned horse or my sister who sometimes lighted in the old stockade cabin, half a mile below. There weren't even fresh tire tracks leading to the judge's cabin.

As usual, I found myself entirely alone on this mountainside with only a cat for company and the ardent persistent determination I entertain to keep loneliness from turning into full-house audience applauding on my solo performance.

A couple of days after Don and Orinda delivered the tanks I go to town and on the way down check the mailbox I share with my wayfaring siblings. There is not even a postcard from either indicating their whereabouts. Since I decided to finish a bear-proof studio alone and figured to do the same with the bathhouse, I hadn't contacted Jim for help. So there would be no reply from him. There was only the weekly Bi-Mart advertisement inside and I left it there.

"Hi Lavon." Del stops wedging sticker stock between layers of one-by to greet me as I step out of my truck at his one-man sawmill.

"Hi Del." His real name is Delbert, the two-syllable pronunciation sounding too drawn out for cordial exchanges between people who are tuckered out by long work days and short paychecks.

Del looks the same as when I'd last seen him—whisker stubble rough as the boards he planes, sawdust powdering his worn flannel shirt and jeans. Over winter he'd lost another tooth from his heartwarming smile, but not another finger to a saw blade.

It takes two trips to haul all the one and two-by I bought to build the bath-house walls. Loaded to the gunwales, Tank could have lugged the entire batch with room to spare.

On the way back from Taynton's mill to buy lumber, I stop again at the mailbox. The weekly Bi-Mart insert—the nearest discount outlet is in Ontario, 130 miles east—is covered by a white envelope.

Decisively typed, the letter informs me that part of the pod of relatives I'd been developing a case against since I was seventeen, to sue for embezzling from my trust fund, have moved out of the country to manage an affiliate family business. Therefore, I would need to hire another attorney experienced in international law as my attorney in Minnesota is not.

"Arrgghh!" I yell instead of swearing and slam my fist onto the mailbox; the hollow sound of boney flesh upon alloy adds bass to my higher-pitched caterwauling.

On this deserted roadside my voice would carry to the rooftops, one in particular, two miles back—a building site behind a greatly-diminished plywood pile that is crawling with shirtless six-pack and beer-bellied roofers. If I resorted to raging vulgarity it might startle them off the peak, so I just repeat "Arrgghh! Arrgghh! Arrgghh!" and beat up the mailbox.

I re-read my attorney's letter attached to an invoice which reignites the white-hot anger I felt at having to pay out thousands of dollars to seek justice that would never settle around me like the dust I was kicking up. Though I was no longer a minor, a ward of the state, I was back to where I started when I first initiated this legal recourse—pissed-off at being ripped-off.

Propriety be damned as me! "Fuuuuck!" I yell loud enough to drown out the roofer's distant hammering.

I rise to a crescendo, squalling out the monosyllabic obscenity, noting it as an adjective, verb and noun, referencing persons, places and things in sentences I spew in time with the beat of a nice round rock on the mailbox.

"Fuuuuuuuuuuuuuuuck!" I roar a booming grand finale loud enough to jingle ice cubes in glasses of gin and tonics clutched in the hands of passengers seat belted in the jet overhead. If I could jump high enough, I'd grab hold of its contrail drafting behind like a gauzy ribbon—or soaking toilet paper, depending on one's metaphorical perspective. I'd hang on until that flight touched down in a place where I didn't have to think about embezzling relatives, marauding bears, wood burners or board feet.

But solidly grounded in my fury, fantasizing over an escape, is getting me nowhere but sweaty and sunburnt at a rural road intersection. I wad up the Bi-Mart ad along with my attorney's bill to use as tinder, that invoice igniting a heat of its own if not properly addressed.

It took as long for me to lay the bathhouse roof as it did to lay up four walls because of all that climbing on a twelve-foot ladder I blocked and double checked each time I scaled it. Finished, the roof peaks at eight feet leaving plenty of clearance over the tanks.

Although I had no idea what I needed to vent the contents of a burning barrel, the clerk at True Value did and I walked out of the hardware store with six-inch stovepipe, an elbow and cap but no flue and three twenty-two-foot-long hoses. And they weren't even on sale. Exchanging cash with the clerk is the societal high of my week.

I assemble the pipe and run it up through a key-hole-sawed opening in the roof, then flash around it with some tin sheeting liberated from one of Don Paulsen's sundry piles. Topped off with leftover tar paper and shakes, that roof shelters the greatest luxury I've known on this mountain—a hot bath.

Late that same day I screw the hoses together and drag them up the creek far enough, I hoped, to create a gravity flow all the way to the bathtub. I kneel on a boulder then lift another to anchor one end of the hose down in the freezing water—a twisted maneuver that face-plants me into the creek and sends the hose downstream. Hung up on a snag, the length sways flaccidly back and forth like a water snake until I haul it back upstream and anchor one end down again with a beefier boulder.

The expected flow out of the other end of the hose results in less than a dribble. I shake it then stick the coupling in my mouth, drawing in and blowing out the way I'd once seen my father siphon motorboat gasoline.

Puffing and sucking away until I'm as blue in the face as the air around me and jumping about like Mick Jagger, I can't get any satisfaction as much as I try. On top of hyperventilating, now I have to get the image of a misogynist mophead out of my mind.

Finally, my efforts produce a drip. Then a trickle. A hiccup and rush that gives in to a steady flow.

I stick the hose into the upper barrel bung and listen to the stinging ring of it filling. Then build a fire in the bottom barrel and keep it stoked and crackling. In twenty minutes the upper tank is full and an hour later the water roiling. I drape the rose-colored hose over the side and twist open the spigot. As the tub fills I retrieve shampoo and soap in the cabin, anticipating a luxurious soaking.

When I return the tub is filled with what looks like an elongated plating of tomato soup. The barrel's rusted insides boiled free, garnishing the red water with flakes of metal. I pull the plug and leave the tank hose to drain. My hygiene that day a blundering plunge in the creek.

The next two days I fill, empty and refill the upper tank, flushing out the last clingy corrosion flake. On the third day I build another fire and soak that night in hot water clear as the cold source. Enough hot water for three satiated rinsings. More than enough water left to wash a few dishes left drying in the moonlight.

Building the bathhouse took time away from my drawknifing. But a daily dose of ardent and persistent determination is the cure-all to skinning through that log pile. In the first month back on the mountain I manage to debark every log slick as jelly. But the urgency to lay them up into a bear-proof studio is gone thanks to the bears. Unlike summers before, I've yet to see even one of them. Something clatters around the cabin well after the kerosene lamps have been blown out and I figure it must be the Godzilla of pack rats because in the morning instead of claw marks or paw prints I see poop pellets on the porch. Still, I take Boo-Boo to bed with the safety off.

24. Workload

It takes an entire workday, 8 a.m. to 4 p.m., to push, pull, and roll four peeled sill logs down to the building site and set them in place. Since they are the largest diameter logs, they are also the heaviest and hefting them onto the foundation is back-breaking, ovary-bursting work, To get hand-drilled holes to fit over rebar shafts cemented into the wall is even more challenging. Precision has never been my middle name and I spend hours re-drilling and adjusting the orifices to mate.

This summer I'm lucky if I can get a full tier laid in one day. Notching does not come back to me as naturally as riding a bike after some time out of the saddle. My building acuity is as reduced as my muscles grown flaccid during nine months of lifting nothing heavier than sculpting tools or paint brushes.

As backbreaking as it is to get a log from the pile down to the site it is even more grueling to get a log up on the rising foundation. I bend at the knees, squat and cradle the biggest butt end, puff out my cheeks, power lift the log and wedge a wood scrap to block the end to keep it from rolling off. Repeat the process on the other end until the log is parallel to the one below. By the end of a work day my Herculean feats leave me a quivering sack of meat, my lower spine as flexible as the rebar shafts I sledge every two feet to stabilize slowly rising walls. Nor is Jim around to eyeball my mistakes or to tell me how much more or less I have to notch away. Blind ambition guides me until I get each notch to sit tight.

I mail-order a curved adze from a fancy wood-working catalogue, thinking it will aid my chiseled refinement, only to discover my only whetstone is flat so trying to keep it razor sharp is pointless. Besides the Echo, that highfalutin adze is one of the few tools I've purchased brand new. Because it was expensive I feel bound to use it, dull or not.

Four days into July I am able to notch only two logs because the Echo sputters and dies out in the middle of a cut. Then I must climb down from the log I'm straddling, yank it to a start and haul it hand over hand up from the ground on the other end of a green nylon rope. By late afternoon I'm limp as the rope, grimy as the carburetor I screw apart to adjust and read-just until the chainsaw is able to sustain a steely a breath.

That night while sharpening the adze, I imagine myself at a barbeque, sparklers in hand, revering Fourth of July festivities amid a beer-guzzling crowd. Instead, I celebrate my independence by staring at a pine cone as it bursts in a fire heating my wash water. Too worn out to build a fire in the bath-house, I'll have to make do with sponging off the pitch blemishing my exterior. The rest of the week is about as fulfilling.

On Tuesday, the peeve hook snaps out from the log I've been dogging, rolling over my thighs and thrusting me backwards to the ground.

On Wednesday, the chainsaw's piping muffler grazes my calf, charring the skin to bacon.

On Thursday, while carrying a raft of fresh-split stove wood, fir slivers pierce through my tank top into my breasts.

By Friday, July 9th, I blow up like the fireworks I didn't have to celebrate a nation's declaration. My smoldering frustration enlightens the evergreen environment with red-hot words every time I pull the chainsaw cord. Even after I clean and gap its plug, it only sparks a start then chokes out after a cut or two. When the Echo finally farted out I ranted on so much that Western Tangiers fled in premature migration.

In the company of a cold chainsaw I bawled my brains out.

25. Research

Despite the pains, frustration and endless hours where my soul chant is *woe is me*, I like working on this little cabin all alone and paying for my mistakes instead of paying for hired help. It's one hundred percent more challenging but as equally fulfilling to have only myself to praise or to blame. I push beyond those points where I think I can push no further. Charge on until I champion a challenge. When this fails, I scuffle with defeat. Then it's tempting to give up. Throw in the towel. Sit in the corner. Light a cigarette. Have a drink. But I'm not a smoker and if I toasted every one of my failures I'd be perpetually drunk, clean out of dry towels and always have my back against a corner.

When confronting an undertaking that feels at the start insurmountable, I approach it from different angles until I frame a dogleg fit then get to work. If my old friend Failure starts tapping me on the back, I try to shrug her off. If that doesn't work I swear and launch a tantrum along with rocks and sticks until I'm drained of piss. It's a performance I perfect with every log I pull, push and cuss into place.

By the end of July my slow, excruciating progress shows in log walls taller than me. With two rounds higher to go before I can lay the loft floor, I decide to take the morning off to paint a sprig of Indian paintbrush. As I stand on the cabin porch, mixing oil colors over a fresh canvas my mind wanders from the *Zen of Seeing*, to the nagging voice of What I Should be Doing.

Instead of painting a wildflower I should take Inipi to the vet to update his vaccinations. I should get a haircut, go grocery shopping, do laundry and check the mailbox because I am low on fire starter.

Instead I take up with a juicy outburst of cadmium oranges, reds and yellows. By noon I've synchronized a riot of paint on gessoed linen. Knowing when to back off, I quit the painting before I kill its spirit. To keep my inspiration from dying too I fill a mug with water, take a sip for myself then set the bloom inside.

In Mendocino I bought a tattered copy of *The Science of Knowing,* by Rudolph Steiner, its pages still smelling like the bookstore, an aromatic blend of cedar, incense, other smoking matter, garlic and mildew. As I clean my brushes I prop the book open with a piece of stove wood and read:

"Tantric Indian thought holds that each and every shape, color, object, and action in the world is a visible form of vibrational level of primal thought that exists beyond the sensate mind. These visible forms of vibrational levels, like symbols, are capable of infinite combination and arrangement, giving rise to the innumerable nuances of knowledge."

I'd never come across tantric before but it reminded me of Titanic. Though the two words shared the phonic form of a fated ship and the last vowel and consonant, their meaning didn't share a similar ending.

If tantric was practiced by the Cayuse, long ago departed from a meadow where I still find obsidian arrow heads, then that tribe must have left vibrations behind in the wildflowers I pick there because I could feel the Indian paintbrush sprig in a tin cup cry out, "I'm wilting." It's a perennial rapport I've developed since the first time I sliced into a tree.

I re-read the part about vibrational levels with a sinking feeling because I knew what Steiner was talking about. I was on the same wavelength with each stick, stone, pine cone, this mountain's every haling breath, wary that everything I touch becomes a part of me. Cognizant that by immortalizing that sprig of Indian Paintbrush on canvas meant I was also crucifying it.

I hadn't left the mountain for nearly two weeks and my inclination to commune with oil paints and wild blooms was overpowered by necessity. But I shied from getting near enough to an engine to feel it turn over and the propelling drive ending at places with razor-sharp intersections and electric simulated lighting enclosing things that poked and sheared and slots that sucked silver coins from my fingers.

I put off going to town. One more day wouldn't jeopardize my cat's immunity. No one was around to scrutinize my long stringy locks. One clean shirt remained folded in a drawer.

That night, sitting before a fire kindled from turpentine-smeared Bi-Mart ads, I ate the remaining cheese and last apple. A wet oil painting hung on a nail in the log wall behind the stove. Earlier I had replanted the subject matter in a meadow under a sky now black as an obsidian arrow.

After a necessary trip to town, Jim drives up five days later in response to a mailed note asking for help. Working in tandem we erect rustic scaffolding, enabling me to work higher and more safely. Without his help that day it would have taken me three or four times longer to build scaffolding from two-by-eights, sixteen feet off the ground, then haul up eight logs for later notching.

After he has packed up his tools and driven away there is still enough daylight for me to continue what we started. But I am tired of notching. Instead I go down to relax by the creek. Legs spread long, propped up on ashy elbows, I am nearly eye level with a jam of branches and sticks damming the shallow stretch of my bathing pool, brainless water striders skimming the surface.

Swimming bugs didn't bother me but the snake that poked out of the dam while I was bathing yesterday did. I take off my work boots, walk into the deepest part of the pool. Limb by limb I bust apart the jam, dam-packing sediment flushing fast downstream. In a flash the bathing pool flows clear giving me pause to worry over how many water bugs I orphaned. Maybe they'd find foster homes days later, sheltered in the silty John Day riverbed.

After playing bad beaver there's still plenty of daylight left to take a hike with Inipi. He doesn't seem to suffer too notably from his last vaccine. During the process he twisted out of the vet's hold with the needle still in hind quarter when he hit the floor—an accident that has added a little giddy-up to his pattering hitch. I slow my pace to account for his.

In a high meadow we stop to study a weathered deer kill surrounded by lady slippers. Pixy pale purples fringe the pelvis of an ungulate now fertilizing viridian range it once grazed. When I stretch out to get a worm's eye view of this boney layout, Inipi does too.

We lie there, side by side, the thunderous valley back dropping the kill, and I massage his hobbled thigh under a pelt silkier than the grass prickling my underside. Hair strands tickle my mid-back, I think, until my scratching hand discovers the itching is not freshly trimmed hair but red ants. I stand, brush away the pests and ascertain my bearings as I plan to return to paint this decomposition.

During all this observing I have been counting seconds—*one thousand one, one thousand two*—calculating how long it will take for the storm brewing in the valley to boil up to this mountain.

One thousand three… On four the cracking lightning signals it is time to head for shelter. To hasten our retreat from the tempest advancing, I sling Inipi around my neck like the mink stole I remember my mother wearing or like the lamb on Jesus' shoulders pictured in my catechism book.

By the time we reach the porch, the forest has whipped into a sleety primal dance foreshadowing what is in store and the elegant fur or little lost lamb draping my neck is really a gimpy feline now dripping wet. By the time I've toweled off Inipi and piled enough wood on the porch to keep a fire burning all night, heaven has pulled the plug and it is raining cats and dogs.

I pour a mug of cheap wine, wishing it was Scotch, instead then fill a bowl with kibble for Inipi. He ignores it, distracted by a little brown mouse who's scooted up through the floorboards. Together they play a disadvantaged match of cat and mouse in the spotlight of two kerosene lamps, Inipi batting the fur puck back and forth until the vibrational symbols sound the odds in Inipi's favor, signaling I cannot humanely watch from the sidelines any longer.

When I pluck its tail, the mouse attached slips free of Inipi's paws and that cat gives me a look that says, *I'd bitch slap you if I could.* Cupped between my hands the mouse doesn't stir as I nudge the door open and step into a storm whipping my freshly-clipped hair.

Unlike the newborns I'd drowned, this adult has a chance of surviving. After all, he made it past the floorboards, a combatant cat and my good intentions. With the gentleness of an air kiss I place the rattled rodent on the ground and it scuttles away. As I am straightening up, my eyes narrow upon two yellow eyes attached to something standing, sitting or lying about a hundred feet from the steps.

Those eyes don't register a blink as I yell "Aghhhhhhh!" and make a hasty retreat back into the cabin, slamming the door just a moment after a bat flies through it.

Swinging a broom, I chase the flying rat careful to avoid glancing flaming lamps. When the bat is finally whisked out the door, I bolt it closed then sit down to catch my breath. I crack open my journal to write and wonder what Mr. Steiner would say about the vibrational levels stirred.

The inside of the cabin is a mess of books and wood shavings. In between whittling pine boards into shelves to get them to fit snug against curves, I've been reading. Volumes nest on the dining table and chairs, lightly covered in chisel and hand-plane shavings. Books enlighten with subjects new to me, their pages still off-gassing the coastal store where they were bought new and used.

Some of these books, to my pedestrian literary background, contain phrases like, "nadir of materiality" (*15 Color Meditations*) and sentences like, "In this phase the initiating, impulsive Martian energy unites with the basic solar drive for significance" (*Phases of the Moon*). Esoteric terms with far-out meanings require me to read passage after passage over and over to gain a sense of what I'm reading.

Biography of the Earth, by George Gamow, has more words I understand but still I must fumble them into a string of discerning. Boning up on astronomy, I hope, will aide my celestial studies of a satellite body I paint in full phase. I now know:

- The moon's distance from Earth is 386,000 kilometers, or 60 radii of Earth

- The moon's mass is eighty-one times smaller than Earth's

- The moon's age is estimated at four billion years

- The Earth rotates faster than the moon revolves around it, 24 hours against 28 days

- The moon's diameter is 3,476 kilometers

I do not know how a kilometer compares to a mile. I do know it is nearly two miles away from the cabin, this craggy notch of terracotta rock where I read Gamow.

One book, open among others on the dining room table, is all about shapes and their meaning. I sit down beside it and devote two pages in my journal to make notes.

Circle
A universal symbol of wholeness; represents the cycle of the universe, the original, the source and the eventual return to the source. The eye follows the circle in two different ways: by going from the center towards the

circumference, centrifugal movement; by going from the circumference towards the center, centripetal movement.

Spiral

Represents potential center, denoting cosmic forms in motion…is related to lunar animals, water, healing and ecstasy…a schematic image of evolution of the universe, a classical form symbolizing the orbit of the moon, and the serpent.

Cone

Cones are the synthesis of all other shapes.

Crescent

Stands for aspects of change and transformation in the world…linked to water as a representation of the boat and chalice. Together with the star it is a symbol of paradise.

Egg

Eggs correspond to zero or the original void source, the origin and end of all effort, represented by the alchemists' search for the Orphic egg. The egg is also synonymous with the heart as center of the body.

Among other volumes, lying open like stepping-stones leading me to places I can't imagine, is one I've bookmarked with matchsticks and fern leaves. *Hundreds and Thousands: The Journals of an Artist*, by Emily Carr, smells papery new because it is—a rare splurge sought directly and not discovered by serendipity.

Emily Carr writes about what she paints and the loneliness of living alone in the woods to paint; of an even lonelier loneliness she describes when she is out of her element—the wilderness in which she painted.

The only art by Carr I'd seen so far was printed on the jacket cover of her book. It was of old-growth cedar, a composition of conical, spherical, circular arrangements. Movement I thrash around with until it is corralled in my own paintings.

Reading her journal entries I feel a kindred spirit kindling between us, even though she's now a spirit herself as I write in my own, jotting a question mark in the margin beside Orphic egg…because I don't know what one is. I bet if I asked, Chester's could special-order a dozen.

Living at the cabin is like living at the bottom of a tree funnel. I am forever looking up to see slivers of the same light that falls abundantly down upon the commodious John Day valley. I schedule my town trips late afternoon so that on the way I can paint in that golden afternoon glow or, depending on Martian pulses, the full moon. Off a side road named something like Dog, Pine, Indian or Strawberry Creek, I'll set up the French easel in jaded juniper and sagebrush lands and paint until one or the other light sources fades out or I've filled my quota of stretched canvas.

Two mornings in a row I ditch building the studio and drive down to the valley just before sunrise. The light is bluer in the cooler awakening day. Purpled recumbent shadows anchor dewy plant life; moisture evaporates in every rising moment until the skillet-hot sunrise glints off killdeers and magpies rousting. In the pre-dawning I prepare a palette.

On the graveled roadside I rock-jack the French easel legs steady and fasten the canvas. I mix values in accordance with atmospheric perspectives, mate complementary colors, and set up contrasts.

For the next two hours I am a matchmaker of dashes, slashes, bold number 14 brushstrokes and triple 000 fairy-tipped final touches. A rowdy gash of Hooker's Green solicits favors from the proper values of Cadmium Orange and a stately range of Cerulean Blue proceeds into a seamlessly blended sky. Whirling dervish brushes bristle and land on canvas sure as a Baryshnikov The Younger. As I work the composition, color forms emerge configuring a sense of place where methods, materials, mind and spirit settle down, spent as lovers after a first bedding.

I am a visceral painter. If I don't feel something for what I paint I won't paint it. This is why I paint landscapes and not portraits. Although I've completed some for college credit, painting a portrait feels like doing the box step, over and over again, in scuffed brown loafers worn to Saturday afternoon confession. Unlike landscape painting, when I attempt portrait painting I drag my feet. As tentative anatomical features evolve the muse on my shoulder keeps trying to slap a sense into me that by nature I do not have. If you do not recognize the true self you see in the mirror every day, do not ask me to paint your portrait.

Landscape is a different story. Painting on this morning, I grab the muse's hand and we rappel hill and dale with slapstick antics. We fall down

cliff faces, laughing hysterically, and bounce back up precipitous mountain sides after a tumble between valleys bandaged in tangerine and lavender rushings.

In this valley light I am in my element; rendering low-hued rangeland and mountain summits is a primal outlet contrary to my writing where conscripted sentences are linear, indelible black and white cajoled into ABC meaning. Unlike an artist, there is no room for a writer to fool around.

On the second sunrise painting morning, I take a break, turn my back on the canvas and almost step on a half smashed snake. Keeled scales and fine fish-like bones lace into the gravel shoulder. Despite its grisly posture the snake retains a dolphin grin cupped toward a sky diffusing aromas of yesterday's haying. I toe the head until the Panglossian smile is upturned like a rainbow leached of color and surmise, even before I narrow on its tail, it is a rattler. I further conclude squished roadkill is too gross to include in the foreground of a composition of rolling foothills and cotton-candy-crowned grasses and return to the landscape I'd started before this fated reptilian detour.

I managed to ignore the snake for a while more, but still cannot shake an interest in its tail. After wedging two wet nine-by-twelve-inch oil canvases snug in the truck bed I remove a flat-head screwdriver in the tool kit. This I decide to use instead of the palette knife.

The coast is clear—mill workers, loggers and ranch hands have been on the job since before sunrise. Around here only bankers work banker's hours. Still, I look up and down the road because I don't want a drive-by audience when I stab a stick into the snake's busted-open belly to be double, double sure it isn't faking. Flattened by a tire and pecked apart, its midsection provides the only evidence of damage. Maybe a scavenging red-tailed hawk or a magpie got scared off by the truck that ran over its prey. Or the truck killed it first. Either way, the snake was no threat and going nowhere when I severed its party makers.

August is ticking away fast. There's too much to do around here to be painting cherry-tipped foothills or fooling with roadkill. For the last two weeks of this hottest month on record I focus on working on the studio and battening down the hatches.

One afternoon I build a work bench beneath the main cabin window. I hand-saw two-by-eights on the porch, letting the ends drop to the ground where I also land after absentmindedly stepping on a loose board.

The eight-foot fall is cushioned by scrap lumber, one shard spearing the supple flesh of my left insole. The skin wrinkles when I tug on the piking that remains proud despite all my screaming.

Rhonda, Glen, Don or Orinda could pull it out. But it is my clutch foot and useless to try compressing a pedal to drive to my neighbors for help. I stay seated in the dust and scrap wood, wiggling that mutant sliver back and forth to loosen it, all the while whimpering like a wounded animal. Hammering a six-inch spear clear through my foot was one option that would hurt worse than pulling out the piercing inch. Option two would require a different hand tool than the hammer by my side.

Hobbling under the cabin I grab pliers from the toolbox then prop my foot on the porch step, lean back and in three gut-retching yanks rip that piker out. Rich, red blood wells out of the hole in my insole, spilling unto the dirt and sawdust, making more of a mess than the rattler, only days before guillotined in reverse.

Getting speared by a two-by-four was the last straw.

I threw in the towel.

Unscrewed the pint of whiskey kept on hand for snake bites, poured some over the wound and poured more into me until the sunset doubled.

26. Canine Companion

Roofing did not top my list of priorities but it needed to if I was going to top off my bear-proof studio that summer on the mountain.

But instead of focusing on pitch and rafters my attentions lie with the bear-attracting deer kill, still lying amid wildflowers and after time pretty much cleaned of fur and meat. I'm busy scavenging this skeleton to use in drawings, when movement beyond the scallion swale stiffens my own spine. I know it isn't Buster. That horse is far away on high desert with a brother who has been hired as a full-time ranch hand. I know it isn't Inipi. He's right by my ankles, his whiskers twitching like antenna as I bag kurnled vertebrae and crescent ribs.

That's the moment I decide I need more protection than a gun or a cat. I need a dog. A dog with nose enough to smell out and throat enough to muster up a bark to alert me to or frighten away harm beyond my limited detection, like whatever animal is eyeing me as I pick at this carcass.

Whatever is rustling in the brush beyond those wild onions isn't startled by my presence. But something scares Inipi. He sniffs the air and bolts down slope, waiting for me by the log bridge when I arrive with a bulging burlap bag slung over my shoulder.

Just beyond the bathhouse I shake out the sack atop a colossal ant hill. Over time red ants and their other colored cousins will polish off remaining sinew and the sun will bleach the bones white as baby teeth. Then the bones will be added to my still-life collection along with a deer skull stored in a reconstructed crate. Looking down upon the osseous arrangement, I realize whatever has taken down that deer could also take on me. Leaving the burlap bag to air out by the bank, I wash my hands and drive to town.

On Matt's most recent visit, he told me about a six-month old wire-haired, miniature terrier. He explained it was the remainder of a litter of six eight-week-olds the owner had dropped at the vet clinic where he worked.

"Going to be put down at the end of the week," Matt said to me.

"But I can't have a dog in my apartment in Mendocino." I explained, as he mounted his horse.

Matt turned in his saddle before riding away and added, "If you change your mind, we're not putting him down until Friday."

Now on the drive to town I play *Making a Decision Ping-pong*...to have a dog or not to have a dog, that is the question.

As compassionate as I am for the fate of a pup I've never seen, I don't see how I can help him out. A part-time job, going to college and working to finish my fine-arts certificate at The Mendocino Art Center strained my capacity for caring even for myself. Plus, there is a strict *No Pets* rule at the apartment complex where I live during the academic year.

Between work and schooling, a policy-breaking cat is tribulation enough.

Matt is arranging vaccine bottles in a glass refrigerated case when I enter the vet's office. His job as an assistant there involves caring for anything between the head and tail of any animal massive or minute, mooing or meowing. He seems surprised to see me and stops stocking long enough to lead me out back. Past some empty pens, a lengthy corrugated building is divided into stalls filled with ailing horses and cows.

He stops in front of the only pen without livestock pushing against the rails. All I see behind the gate is a slab of dank concrete and fodder. When Matt unlatches the gate a filthy straw patch escapes.

"Runt of the litter. That's why he's still here." Matt stops the runaway with his boot.

I bend over, brush away hay the color of its mangy fur, pick him up, and at arm's length, soak in an arc he leaks in fear or excitement. Keyed tight as a wind-up toy, that pup strains against a doting grip neither of us is familiar with. When he licks my cheek I can smell what he's been into—a cement cell slick with excrement.

"I'll take him," I tell Matt as the reeking dog piddles some more on my freshly-laundered shirt.

After paying for shots and de-worming medicine, I settle that pungent fur mangle on the Datsun's front seat. He sits silently, staring eye level at the glove box, as I speed through the valley's waning heat ripening the pup's redolent history.

It is too late to bathe him by the time we get back to the cabin. The little dog follows me up the steps and Inipi, defensively poised on the new work bench, watches as the pup jumps and yips in his direction.

Though it takes some time to get the lamps lit and a fire snapping, Inipi still retains his self-guarding arch against a pogo stick puppy. When I smooth his bristled nape he slides me the same look as when I took away his mouse.

"There, there little baby," I say, moving Inipi from the workbench. "Little baby, there, there," I continue consoling as I wedge him by my side in the rocker. The pup at my feet tries to figure out a chair and a lap, solving the question in a jump and is soon wobbling on top of the thigh sheltering a hissing cat.

"You boys will just have to work it out," I explain, petting each simultaneously, a wriggling little dog and pissed-off cat on either side of my lap—a two-handed job that means all the precious ice in my cup of apple juice melts before I have a chance to drink it cold. This peace-keeping process has me wishing for a long drink of room-temp wine instead.

When both animals settle down I rise and make the pup a bed beside the stove before claiming my own. I haven't even blown out the lamp in the loft when that stinky baby wails a whine that would shatter even the world's most stone heart.

Like a football I can't securely forearm, I carry the pup up the loft ladder. The towel he's been crying on beside the stove is smoothed out on the floor next to the bed and I fold in the little dog like taco filling.

"It's just for one night," I promise Inipi who is already curled by my pillow. I haven't even blown out the lamp by the time the pup figures out he's more comfortable sleeping cheek to cheek.

"It's just for one night." I plead as Inipi darts off the bed and heads to the ladder. Arching his head over a jack-knifed haunch before clawing down, he gives me a look I am familiar with by now.

Though I keep pushing him away, that pup is intent on becoming best buddies with my face. I reluctantly placate a need for warmth and connection that has been brewing since he was pulled from his mother's teat and deposited in a cattle pen. I resign myself to sharing the night with his embedded and scruffy-haired orphaned fetor.

In the morning, as soon as a triple portion of wash water is heated, I scrub my face and chest then the pup twice in Johnson's Baby Shampoo; dry him with the old towel he wouldn't sleep on.

All morning that pup follows me about as I work on the bear-proof studio. By afternoon Inipi, who is still bent from his place, assumes his station in the hierarchy, sticking to my heels; both animals are tied close as shoe laces to my every step. By evening they are best of pals, and playfully chasing pine cones I throw over their furry heads.

That night in the rocker, each assumes his place on either side of my lap, Inipi purring, the pup sighing. There is still ice in my apple juice cup when I tackle the ladder one handed.

In bed, I stretch out straight, a baby dog on one side, a prepubescent cat on the other. I am the motherly filling, sandwiched between a little family in the making.

Before I blow out the lamp, the sleepy pup is named Arthur.

A week after Arthur came into play I was running through the judge's meadow, the pup dwarfed by calf-high grasses, when I saw Mark's truck bending the road below. We met at the fork, a stretch before his truck was to confront the Eliminator. That's where I introduced Arthur to my brother by lifting the puppy, panting, up to the cab window.

"Here's your mail." Marks flinty steel eyes flare as he holds out a Bi-Mart flier. I can't grasp it with Arthur substantially in my grip. The paper feathers down to the dirt as Mark adds, "I'd shoot that dog if I had a gun in my hand right now."

Fortunately, he does not open the glove compartment hosting a handgun arsenal before he shifts and floors it. Pebbles stings my ankles as my brother revs up ruts. During our brief exchange Mark didn't divulge if he was still employed as a ranch hand or if he would be staying in the rat shack, nor had I ventured to ask. Nor would I ever go near my brother again when I was with the pup I named after our father.

27. Positive Ions

I wish the idea of a bear-proof studio had remained just that. I'd rather be painting than whacking away with a hammer or ax. My cash stash, devoted to stocking up on canvases and oil paints to see me through the summer, is almost too depleted to cover building materials. To finish what I started means draining my financial reserve to the very bottom to pay Jim to help with ridgepole and rafters. Weeks before ordering roofing, he had wisely revised my crude architectural rendering by calculating a steeper pitch to make it easier for snow to slide off. It takes days of angling two-by-fours before the roof is ready for boards.

To save money I lay the roof by myself, cutting eight-foot sections instead of twelve-footers. Just the loss of four-feet makes hauling up boards and crow barring them tight that much easier, though the pitch is so steep I have to tie myself around the waist, the other end around a log for safety.

Metal roofing is less aesthetic than the tamarack shakes I used on the cabin, but it offers better protection against potential wildfire. With Jim's help I calculate how many sheets I will need and telephone in an order to a supply store in Boise, mailing them a check that includes the cost of delivery. The delivery gets as far as the judge's meadow. After one look at the Eliminator the driver's chicken choice delegates me as the hauler of panels extending past the Datsun's bed. He drives away after leaving his load at the foot of the most challenging piece of road, not even offering a refund for the service he'd been pre-paid to deliver.

Hoisting galvanized aluminum sheeting in and out of a truck bed is a piece of cake compared to lifting a piece up two stories. I wished for another hundred-dollar bill in my boot to pay Jim to help me finish the roof but instead made a withdrawal at the bank.

When Jim arrives, we devise a kind of rope netting to haul up each eight-foot panel. On occasion one slithers out of the improvised harness, crashing to the ground, crumpling at the corners. Tethered by a sixty-foot length of pricey polyester rope, I balance barefooted on steep roofing heating up like a pancake grill and hammer nails with rubber girdles. By noon's mounting sun, my soles fry like bacon and I lace on moccasins as the bottoms of my work boots are too slick to stick on a galvanized incline.

By the time the roof is finished that rope has been stretched to the end and so have my savings.

After the roof was laid it got real quiet on the mountain. Record-high temperatures and gas prices have pretty much confined Anabell and Del Taynton to their air-conditioned house. Even Don Paulsen's nightly howdy-dos have subsided. Three days horizontal on the couch might have been long enough for him to heal sufficiently to stand upright but being anciently run over by his John Deere has severely limited his mobility. Mark, who alighted at the rat shack, departed only days after being introduced to a dog with a name that roused his *Lost boy sleeping in a bed of stomach ulcers.*

I usually balance isolation with work. Not since the very first night I moved into the cabin and realized that I was too empty to fill it, have I felt this unaddressed dark hollow. It resides smack in my chest, a visceral chasm that makes me gag on food I can't swallow.

All I can manage to down is coffee, water and apple juice to fill the pit I want to scorch with Scotch straight from a bottle that I would buy if I could force myself to drive to town where being around people would likely make me hit rock bottom.

For two days I stay on the porch and paint, glancing down the road between ponderous brush strokes, hoping someone will walk up, stop dead in their tracks and take an impartial gander at this odd bird; maybe offer an outstretched hand to bridge wild falter and mortal connection. Only stingy breezes and stinky memories make the trek.

While on occasion my mind can get a bit mussed, I'm a steadfast stickler about keeping my quarters tight as hospital corners. To see an object, even as innocuous as a soup spoon, out of place is enough to founder my collinear sense of order. My mind, on the other hand, has clutters and caches of recollections purposely swept into corners. Like dust bunnies, some get kicked up by contemplative winds over a past where things were openly out of place.

My feelings of displacement began at birth. I squeezed out of my mother's womb into neonatal life five weeks too soon, then was incubated under oxygen compression; a controlled climate lacking in primal loving connections. Antiseptically entombed for days, maybe weeks—I don't recall the whole story—I sucked life inside sterile glass sides scratched by fingers pink as newborn mice.

I grew into a frail child who fell out of trees or off skateboards and bicycles, landing hard in multifarious ways both literal and metaphorical; not because I was clumsy or careless but because of a shifty planet covered with throw rugs that kept getting pulled out from under me.

Major tumbles included not recognizing my father behind a dead-pan stare after his first suicide attempt and the ensuing electroshock therapy sessions that ended his life. Just a few short years later, I had to watch my mother's receding face, white as the sheet draping her body, as orderlies wheeled her away on a hospital gurney toward the losing side of life.

The deaths of my parents led to experiences that scalded away my childhood veneer. Without a family, I fell into a system without safeguards and had experiences that left my insides nicked, scratched and dented and filled me with unshed tears.

The feelings of displacement ratcheted up when I had time to think back on the conditions and circumstances of my adolescence. I was touched in ways minors should never be touched, actions I believed at the time were caring and consensual. Now, as a young adult, I realize they were neither.

It's this last pearl in my string of thinking that makes me sick. Maybe this cabin is a log incubator. And the mountain is the tending day nurse. And the creek is really a purging enema.

While I flounder with memories and paint on the porch, Inipi and Arthur stay inside, curled together in the rocker, shying from my stinky think. After two days of reflective reverie my melancholy has leaked into bruising blue canvases and my pets don't move a whisker when I leave the porch.

I walk alone to the creek and plant my easel on the bank beside a frothing whirlpool and scrutinize values that won't cease lashing, chutes laddering down splashy rock faces. The last time I stood so reverently beside this spot I was in the company of a baby bird on a branch and a realtor in a cowboy hat.

Harnessing this cascading alabaster ruckus of milky glacial run-off forces me to lighten up the shadowy palette I'd been brushing out in the previous two days of forest painting. I squeeze out a mass of Titanium then blend up patches mixed with tads of Naples Yellow, Payne's Grey; just enough to tone down splurging creek highlights so they remain brilliant but not falsely overpowering.

In Mendocino I developed these blends in order to paint the crashing ocean, stuffing custom mixes into empty tubes labeled, *Reflected Light, Refracted Light, Absorbed Light.* Each time I painted the sea I felt better than before and sought out a book that might explain why I felt soothed after painting white-capped rampage. I found one explanation concerning the atomic relationships in moving water in a used physics textbook: negative ions.

I always thought of a negative ion as a pessimistic microscopic speck. But this musty textbook said they were atoms charged with electrons. Instead of possessing a bad attitude they can produce mood-enhancing biochemical reactions in the body and mind; alchemy stirred by moving water.

Continuing my pseudo-science research in Mendocino led me to invent a wave catcher to further my investigation of negative ions. Actually it was a plastic Clorox jug with the top cut off and a long wiry clothesline tied to the handle. But I called it my wave catcher because that's what it did.

The first wave I caught was on a full moon night. From an outcrop on the coastal headlands I unfurled the contraption, the jug biting into the tip of a wave just before it broke against the sandstone bluff where I stood firmly at the other end of the clothesline. Hand over hand I pulled up the jug filled with a wave tip sloshing around inside. In the studio I dipped my brushes into the wave catcher, using the water as a vehicle to charge acrylic paint across canvas.

Since returning to the cabin that summer, I'd forgotten about the healing powers of moving water, even though it was rushing all around my land. It never even occurred to me this glacial mountain mineral stream could emulate a thrashing salted sea.

I move the easel to work on the creek bank, dipping my brushes directly into the wild water below a boulder where I'd once retrieved a bloody rib bone and later observed a water ouzel. I paint acrylic studies until I run clear through my canvas supply, then resort to washes on paper. I don't really like working in acrylic paint, especially on paper. But using atomically charged creek water as a medium necessitates this conveyance. Sorry gray-fused shadows on canvas are transformed into brilliant blue flushings on paper.

I am still living on coffee, water and apple juice, a diet, day by day reducing the physical matter between me and the subject I paint. Three days sustained only by liquid leaves me shaky and clearly much lighter. By the fourth day I'm done with painting and like silt piled behind a boulder, bit by bit my mental murk has washed free. The sprites return to my cells sure as smolts cycle back to their alevin source and I resurface with pluck and an appetite.

"Hey little buddies," I join Inipi and Arthur who've roused from the rocker to greet me on the porch and their eyes open wide as I unlatch the cooler. The three of us sit in a sun swatch sharing bite-sized Tillamook cubes pared with my Girl Scout knife.

"One for you, one for you, and one for me," I promise, doling out uniform cheese chunks.

Arthur wolfs his.

Inipi nibbles.

I chew mine behind a waxing smile.

When the cheese is finished Inipi grooms his whiskers and Arthur lies beside me as I stretch my legs on the porch and write in my journal.

Journal Entry August 26

There is a reality embedded in the cracks below the surface of convention, of material goods, of interpersonal communication. It is the reality out of the hubhub, rooted in the quiet way the heart turns, seeking to explore its nature in solitude, in nature.

This reality takes shape, gives voice in the findings after the digs of self-examination. It is a conscious and unconscious exploration of the self, an examination of the dreams that mount up in the mind.

One must fall into this crack, or step knowingly into it, avoid the trample of society, in order to hear, see, feel the body and spirit we were born with.

There is a life in ourselves we rush by in our search for fulfillment, fortune, love. I find this self, the primal one, only through living in a blast of solitude that can be as easy to swallow as it is often difficult to digest. It is in this living in and from myself that I grow the most.

This self finds ecstasy in winds whipping trees, in the waver of trout against the earthly mosaic creek bottom, in the attitudes of the domestic and wild animals that live with me. It is the essence I seek that nurtures this solitude. It is only here that I find what lies beneath the fast churn of outer progress.

It is ominous, coldly lonely, intensely refreshing to live this life between the cracks. It is not only a time to feel the richness of silence, but a time for self reflection. When I reach a point of clarity, then I know I am seeing through the filters of experience that have created patterns I act and react from.

I close the journal, walk into the cabin, grab the broom and continue to sweep out dusky corners.

28. Self Portrait

The latest Blue Mountain Eagle advertises a clothing sale at Alec Gay Hall. My denim and flannel glad-rags broadcast my proclivity for investing in hand tools over highbrow outfits, but it's time to spruce up my wardrobe. In just a week this summer on the mountain will draw to a close and I will be back to working in deadline and official paper places where jeans and flannels remain in the closet.

I haven't left the mountain during my days of brooding and the opportunity to exchange words with strangers while wrestling with new vestments seems fitting. My paint stock could get me through another month or two but my food supply won't last the week and needs replenishing.

"See you later little buddy." I kiss Inipi goodbye and close the cabin door on the whisker slicker in the rocker.

"Load up," I direct boinging Arthur and he springs into the cab and skids across the bench seat to ride shotgun.

Shopping that day includes groceries, a stop at the hardware store for a pick, duct tape, molding strips and a new chain for the saw. But even more extravagant is buying city clothes. I pull up in the shade of Alec Gay Hall, one of many post-gold-rush, post-World War II stone buildings patterning John Day's eclectic architecture. Today the dimly lit interior has been transformed into a spread-out trunk sale. Fold-out tables are stacked and portable racks hang with new clothing one or two years out of style. The clothes are all shiny, starchy and chemically smelling—not time-worn like the Goodwill jeans and shirts that trail sweet Cheer until I wear them out in the pitchy woods and around puffing wood fires.

The changing room is a section of the hall draped off by blankets hung from ropes. This communal changing area conceals gaggles of women squirming in or out of old fashions. I have no compunctions running around the mountain bare-breasted but behind the blankets I blush with modesty as I try on blouses.

When I dress again in my jeans, checkered shirt and work boots, I look again like I do not fit in. The women around me casually wear clothes like the sprightly slacks and floral-patterned vestments I have only bought to appear professional and proper.

"Move little buddy." Arthur smells the plastic bag filled with new duds. I stow them next to fresh groceries behind the seat before driving to Prairie City.

Del is in the saw shed when I park in the lumber yard beside layers of boards I helped him sticker stock a month before. I wait until he is done ripping through a log before waving. Startling him as he is sawing might make him take his eye off the blade and I don't want any part of responsibility for his losing another finger. When the log is sliced I step into Del's view. He flicks a switch and the din dies down until the saw blade is still and silent. That's when I approach the shed and say, "I want to buy some planed two-by."

Del has me repeat the question and I stand in front of him this time, because now he can only really hear clearly if he can see your lips moving. He says he doesn't have any finished lumber on hand. If I help him though, he'll plane rough-cut into the shelving I want.

First the space under the planer has to be cleared. I spend half an hour shoveling curlicue shavings into a rickety wheelbarrow and emptying it in the teepee burner's belly while Del tools about gauging the blades. When we finally get those boards moving, the planer is so screamy I can't hear Del but can only read his lips, "Pull." Sawdust clouds the air between us and the plank being shaved.

By four o'clock I have a truckload of sleek boards and a shirt full of itch. I discover, after jumping into the shaving mound I made inside the teepee burner, sawdust is not as gratifying as a tumble in raked maple leaves. By half past four I am splashing away this failed childhood memory of a Midwest fall. Earlier that month, I'd uncovered a shady spot off the highway by the river and promised myself I would return to paint the plateau view across that shore.

The location is just far enough off the highway so I am undetected by passing traffic. It also offers a clear upland view of open cattle range and is

166

close enough to a cottonwood grove that I can climb low branches if those boundary-less bovines decided to stampede.

It is also a good place to give Arthur his first swimming lesson. He'd been patient all day while I girly-shopped and milled. I release him in the river's middle and dog paddle beside him until we scamper ashore. Then I treat him to a small tin of wet dog food, a delicacy he'd never enjoyed before and he laps up the entire can of mush I mashed with a stick on a flat boulder. While he digests, I dry in my underpants and paint in the fringe of cottonwood shade.

A knobby mix of sienna is swept and stippled to form a crazed sedimentary formation onto a seamless blended manganese sky. I move between painting high mesa and lower river washboard, tippling highlights, angling cast shadows and anchoring precise rock bottom reflections.

When I think I am finished with what I started, I step back from the easel. Close one eye. Narrow the other on the monolithic geological upheaval looming down upon, or hovering above—depending upon your philosophical viewpoint—a water bed patterned with pebbles that have been rolled about, roughed up and smoothed by seasonal highs and lows.

I open the shut eye then focus both. Scrutinize the canvas long enough to title it, "Self Portrait."

The End

CPSIA information can be obtained
at www.ICGtesting.com
Printed in the USA
BVHW050549140723
667188BV00003B/11

9 781737 459118